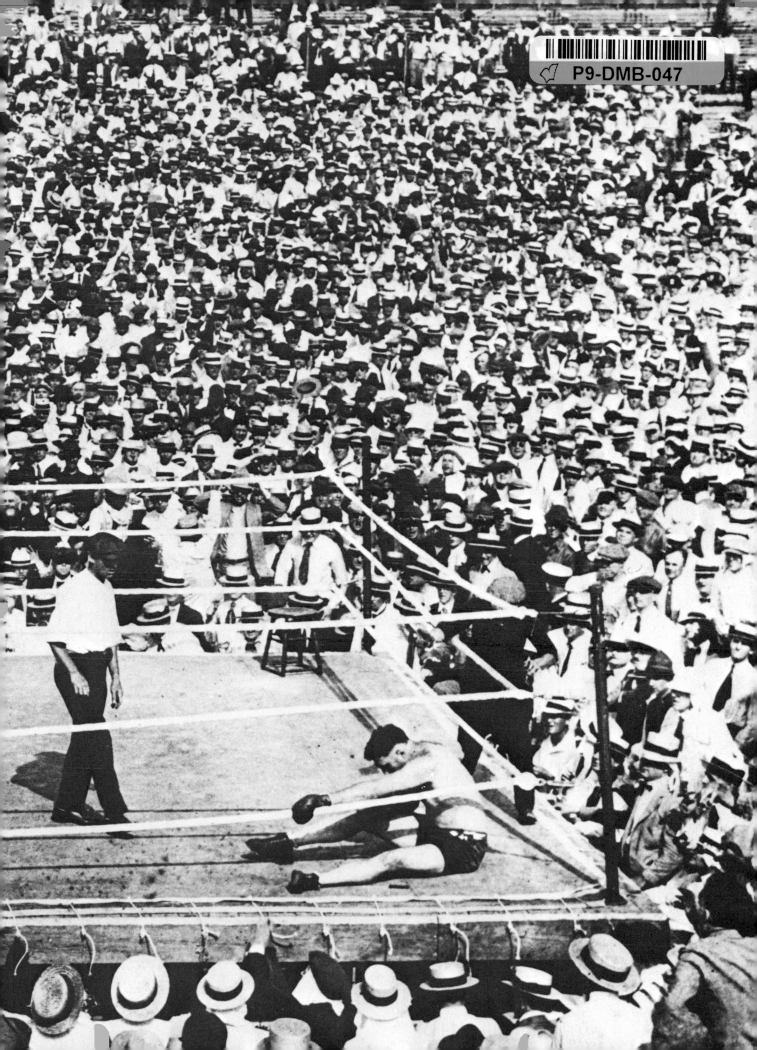

Great moments in American sports

Exciting accounts of the games that made history and the stars who became national celebrities from the turn of the century to the present. From the first Rose Bowl game in 1902 to Hank Aaron's record-breaking homer in 1974, the high points of sports history come alive. More than 150 photographs.

illustrated with photographs

Great moments in American sports

BY JERRY BRONDFIELD

Random House · New York

PHOTOGRAPH CREDITS: A.F.P. from Pictorial Parade, 118 bottom; Bettmann Archive, 14 left, 20, 23 top and bottom, 25, 26, 27, 29 left, 30, 34, 52, 55 right, 74; Brown Brothers, 21, 33, 38, 39, 41 right, 46, 47, 48, 62, 73 left, 104; Canada Wide from Pictorial Parade, 88; Rich Clarkson, 122 bottom; Culver, 35, 37, 44, 64; Malcolm W. Emmons, 130; Indianapolis Motor Speedway, 31; Frank Lennon from the Hockey Hall of Fame, 59; Library of Congress, 15, 28, 29 right; National Aeronautics and Space Administration, 110 left; New York Historical Society, 40; New York Yankees, 43, 78; Photography, Inc., 136; Pictorial Parade, 122 top; RCA, Inc., 95 left; Ken Regan/Camera Five, 108, 133; The Smithsonian Institution, 14 right; Tournament of Roses, 16, 17; United Press International, endpapers, reverse of front endpaper (right), 1, 2 bottom left and right, 5, 13 left and right, 41 left, 51 top and bottom, 55 left, 56, 58, 60 left and right, 61 left and right, 66, 67, 68 left, 71, 75, 79, 81 right, 82, 83, 84, 85, 86, 90, 92 left and right, 93 left, 94, 97, 98, 101 bottom left, 107, 110 right, 112, 114, 115 right center, right and bottom, 116, 121, 126, 127, 129 left and right, 131, 134, 134–135, 138 top and bottom, 140, 141, 143, 144, 145, 146, 147; U. S. Army, 80–81; U. S. Navy, 80; University of Michigan, 18; Wide World Photos, reverse of front endpaper (left), 2 top left and right, 10, 11, 12, 19, 22, 32, 42, 45, 50, 53, 57, 63 left and right, 68 right, 70, 72, 73 right, 76, 77, 81 left, 87, 89, 93 right, 95 right, 96, 100 left and right, 101 top and bottom right, 103, 106, 109, 110–111, 113, 115 left and left center, 118 top, 120, 124, 132, 135, 139; John Zimmerman, LIFE Magazine, © Time Inc., 125.

COVER: Melchior DiGiacomo, left center (Billie Jean King); Neil Leifer for SPORTS ILLUSTRATED, © Time Inc., bottom right (Mark Spitz); Ken Regan/Camera Five, top left (Joe Namath) and bottom center (Bill Russell and Wilt Chamberlain); United Press International, bottom right (Joe Louis and Max Schmeling); Wide World Photos, top right (Lou Gehrig and Babe Ruth).

Library of Congress Cataloging in Publication Data
Brondfield, Jerry, 1913–   . Great moments in American sports. (Landmark giant, no. 24)
SUMMARY: Describes forty-six great events in United States sports history from the first Rose Bowl in 1902 to Hank Aaron's record-breaking home run in 1974. 1. Sports—United States—History—Juvenile literature. [1. Sports—History] I. Title. GV583.B66 796'.0973
74-4928 ISBN 0–394–82608–6 ISBN 0–394–92608–0 (lib. bdg.)

Cover and text designed by Murray M. Herman

Manufactured in the United States of America   1 2 3 4 5 6 7 8 9 0

For Ruth,
who did
the digging
and the
housekeeping
on a ton
of research
material

Contents

FRONT MATTER PHOTOGRAPHS:

ENDPAPERS: The decisive moment in the 1919 heavyweight championship fight between Jack Dempsey and Jess Willard at Toledo, Ohio.

HALF TITLE PAGES: The first Indianapolis 500 in 1911; Ben Hogan putts in the 1950 U. S. Open golf tournament; Cassius Clay (later known as Muhammad Ali) after fighting Sonny Liston in 1964.

OPPOSITE TITLE PAGE: Swimmer Mark Spitz at the 1972 Olympics; Helen Wills early in her tennis career; Henry Aaron hitting his 715th home run; basketball giant Wilt Chamberlain.

DEDICATION PAGE: Baltimore field-goal kicker Steve Myhra ties the 1958 NFL championship game, sending it into sudden-death overtime.

Great
moments
in
American
sports

Introduction

The Biggest Home Run

On April 4, 1974, in his first time at bat in the new season, Hank Aaron slams his 714th home run.

It was 9:06 P.M., April 8, 1974. Number 44 for the Atlanta Braves was kneeling in the on-deck circle in Atlanta Stadium. Number 44, of course, was Henry Aaron. Hammerin' Hank. Bad Henry. Enemy pitchers had lots of names for him.

It was the fourth inning. Hank was next up and more fans were watching him in the on-deck circle than were watching Darrell Evans, the man at bat.

The Los Angeles Dodgers were leading, 3–1. Al Downing was pitching. Evans rapped a grounder behind second base. Dodger shortstop Bill Russell jugged it a

moment and Evans was safe at first base.

But never mind all that. A few days earlier, on the opening day of the 1974 season, Hank Aaron had rifled the ball over the left field wall for his 714th home run in the first inning, with his first swing of the bat.

Baseball fans in America—and lots of people who didn't know a baseball from a turnip—knew that Bad Henry had tied the home run record of the great Babe Ruth. And now the question was how long it would take Hank to hit his 715th and break this most famous of records. Perhaps never

Four days later, against Dodger pitcher Al Downing, Aaron blasts number 715, breaking Babe Ruth's "unbreakable" record.

in sports was a number on more people's lips . . . 715.

Sports fans had held Babe Ruth's record of 714 sacred and they had considered it to be unreachable—the only mark in the record book that would be safe forever.

Now here was 40-year-old Hank Aaron getting up from the on-deck circle and advancing to the plate.

Two innings earlier Aaron had walked without getting a single swing at the ball.

More than 53,000 Braves fans had booed the pitcher for not giving Hank something decent to swing at. Millions of fans in a national TV audience felt the same way.

Now Henry Aaron stepped into the batter's box, and the suspense in the stadium began to grow. Downing's first pitch was into the dirt for ball one. The crowd murmured. The second pitch was a fastball. Downing was trying to keep the ball low, but this time he failed.

Bad Henry lashed out with his bat. As his powerful body uncoiled, wood met the ball. A split-second later, the crowd was roaring as the ball sailed in a high arc to deep left-center field. Everyone in the park knew it was going over the wall. Aaron never followed the flight of his hits, but this time, on the way to first base, his eyes followed the ball all the way. He saw Dodger outfielder Bill Buckner leap high against the fence. Buckner didn't have a chance. The ball dropped into the Atlanta bullpen behind the wall.

It was Number 715. Now fireworks were exploding over the scoreboard. Henry Aaron rounded second and third. Already his teammates were waiting for him. As he stepped on home plate they surrounded him joyously, shaking his hand and pounding him on the back. It was official. Number 715 was in the books.

Henry's mother and father had jumped out of their box near the Braves' dugout. They raced over to their son. His mother got there first and flung her arms around him.

The game was held up for nine minutes as Henry received awards and best wishes from a half-dozen dignitaries on the field. Atlanta relief pitcher Tom House ran in from the bullpen to hand Henry the ball that had sailed over the left center field wall, the most valuable sports memento in history.

It was a moment that would live as long as baseball is played. And millions of Americans, watching on national TV, were thrilled to share that moment with Henry Aaron, a moment of history, of joy, and of good news.

It was a fitting addition to the dozens of other special moments that have made millions of Americans devoted followers of sport.

After circling the bases, Hank is lifted to his teammates' shoulders. Moments later he gets a big hug from his mother.

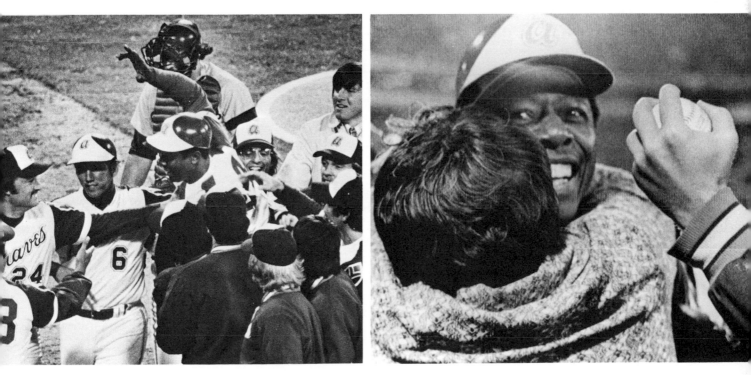

As America entered the Twentieth Century, it was still a young nation carving out its destiny—exploring new ideas and settling new lands. Oklahoma, Arizona and New Mexico were not yet states. The Panama Canal had not yet been built, and if you wanted to sail from New York to San Francisco you had to go all the way around South America.

The telephone was still a new invention. In rural areas, phone service was often non-existent. The nearest hospital might be 200 miles away. Radio was just a dim dream in the future. There were no movie theaters, no public golf courses and no public tennis courts.

Detroit was just beginning to turn out early, undependable automobiles. In many towns an auto had not yet been seen. Paved roads were almost unheard of, and horses still stood at hitching posts on the main streets of the country.

America was still largely an agricultural nation, and people stayed close to home. They worked long hours, and their pleasures and pastimes were mostly home-grown. But gradually, more leisure time was becoming available, especially in the cities and towns. And people were discovering sports. The average American, perhaps because of his frontier heritage, found physical games a natural outlet for his energy. Either as a player or a spectator, he found the competition exciting—man against man, team against team, town against town.

In 1900 baseball and boxing were the only sports played by professionals. For college athletes there was competition in track and field, and the Intercollegiate Track and Field Meet was an annual event. In 1900 an American team participated in the second modern Olympic Games at Paris. Baseball's National League was nearly 25 years old, and plans for a competing American League were far advanced.

A turn-of-the-century football uniform . . . the Wright brothers' first flight . . . and war hero Teddy Roosevelt, who became president in 1900.

But on the major university campuses football had replaced baseball as the number one sport. The largest public crowds in America were found at college football games. More than 25,000 fans came to watch games between Harvard and Yale or Princeton and Columbia. At first, big college games were reported in the papers as social events, but soon the coverage began to appear on what the readers would later call "the sports page."

Before long, the sportswriter would become the most widely read reporter on almost any newspaper. The newspapers and the sports fans were helping to create something new on the American scene—the Sports Hero. Celebrity athletes would soon be as familiar to people as presidents or statesmen. No other nation had known anything like the Sports Hero. He was strictly an American invention.

Baseball had already provided the first heroes of national acclaim. In 1890 the Cleveland Spiders (later the Indians) brought up a pitcher named Denton True Young, who was soon nicknamed "Cy" because he threw a baseball that whizzed by as fast as a cyclone. From 1890 through 1899 he won 267 games —an average of nearly 27 a year! Pitching well into the new century, Young won more games (510 in 22 seasons) than any pitcher in history. "Wee Willie" Keeler, an outfielder for the Baltimore Orioles, was well known by most schoolboys. Keeler, the game's first scientific hitter, specialized in poking the ball between the infielders. When asked the secret of his success, he replied, "I hit 'em where they ain't."

Since there was no professional football, the early heroes of that sport were college players, mostly from the East. The greatest gridiron honor was to be chosen to Walter Camp's "All-America team," which Camp had established in 1899. Among the early football giants were Pudge Heffelfinger, Yale's legendary guard; Frank Hinkey, Yale's four-time All-America end; Harvard's halfback, Charley Daly; and a halfback named Isaac Seneca from Carlisle Indian School in Pennsylvania.

Early in the first decade of the new century colorful Teddy Roosevelt, who had won fame in the Spanish-American War, became president after William McKinley was assassinated. In 1903 Henry Ford established the Ford Motor Company, and within a few years he was manufacturing the Model T. That economical automobile would help revolutionize American transportation. Later in 1903 Orville Wright became the first man to fly an airplane.

The world was changing rapidly. And with those changes came some important firsts and some great heroes in sports. As football's appeal spread across the country, the big names were Michigan, Chicago, Stanford and Yale. The first Rose Bowl game was played on January 1, 1902, and the first World Series came a year later. A shortstop named Honus Wagner became the greatest all-around player in baseball, leading his team to four pennants and winning seven batting titles in the decade. And a young Georgian with flashing spikes, named Ty Cobb, was on the way to becoming the first superstar in modern baseball.

The first decade of the 1900s was a peaceful and generally prosperous time —and for sports it was the beginning of an era of national excitement and recognition.

15

1

The First Rose Bowl

Football's most famous game was invented by the most unlikely promoters imaginable —the hotel-owners and businessmen of Pasadena, California.

To understand how unlikely these men were, consider their town. In 1901 Pasadena was a settlement of 3,000 people nestled against the arid mountains of Southern California. It was 15 miles from Los Angeles— then a small city of 100,000. Pasadena had one claim to fame. It was a resort where wealthy people without much to do could spend their winters. In order to promote the town and give paying guests a chance to get out of their wicker rocking chairs, the town fathers had decided to sponsor a Rose Festival. By holding the festival in mid-winter, featuring a lavish parade on New Year's Day, Pasadena could advertise its sunny climate to the millions who were snow-bound that time of year.

But as colorful as the flowered, horse-drawn floats were, the festival didn't seem to come to life. Then in 1901 the festival planners thought of a new attraction to provide a climax for the festivities. They would promote a football game between specially invited teams. The contest would be held in something called "The Rose Bowl," a rather fancy name for the dusty playing field in the Arroyo Seco on the edge of town. (Arroyo Seco means "dry gulch" in Spanish, but none of the publicity would mention that fact.)

But which teams would play? The only nearby college team was the University of Southern California in Los Angeles. Southern Cal had no football reputation at all, and its team played mostly high school teams and rag-tag athletic clubs. The Pasadena boosters were looking for better competition than that.

The best team in the West was Stanford, from Palo Alto, California, 400 miles to the

In Pasadena for the Rose Bowl, Stanford players pose with their cheerleaders.

north. Surely Stanford would draw a crowd among Californians. But who should they play? The Pasadena organizers hoped they could bring in a football power from "the East."

Until 1901 the East in football had meant Harvard, Yale, Princeton, Penn—the schools in the Northeast which had invented and developed the game. But during the 1901 season another team had caught the imagination of football fans. An inelegant team from the University of Michigan had compiled the most amazing record in the land.

The Michigan Wolverines were coached by a young, colorful West Virginian named Fielding H. Yost. In a way, Yost was responsible for both teams in that first Rose Bowl. During the 1900 season he had been the coach at Stanford, and many of the men still on the Stanford team were Yost-trained.

Then in 1901 Yost arrived at Michigan

—with a running back from Oregon named Heston. The Wolverines racked up ten straight victories. And they scored 501 points while their opponents scored none. Averaging 50 points a game (in one they scored 128!), they became known as the "Point-a-Minute" team. Their steam-roller offense gained 8,000 yards, an awesome record never since approached. And their brick-wall defense prevented every opponent from crossing the Michigan 35-yard-line. Could Stanford stand up to such a juggernaut? No one knew, but the Stanford fans felt sure that the stories of the "Point-a-Minute" team were vastly exaggerated.

As New Year's Day approached, the teams arrived from their distant homes. The trip from Ann Arbor, Michigan, took the Michigan team nearly a week by train, and even Stanford had a long, exhausting journey from Palo Alto. Spectators came, too, some from sparsely settled Southern California, others from greater distances.

As the temperature rose toward 90 degrees, the fans in the rose-strewn stands on January 1, 1902, waited impatiently for the Michigan players. They arrived 30 minutes late because they had ridden on one of the Rose Parade floats. The Wolverines had little time to work out before the game, and they started off badly. In fact, for the first ten minutes of the game it looked as if Michigan's reputation was highly overrated. True, Stanford couldn't dent the Michigan defense, but the vaunted Michigan offense was definitely sputtering.

Then, suddenly, eight Wolverines lined up to the right of center with only quarterback Boss Weeks and halfback Willie Heston directly behind. The ball was snapped to Weeks, who pitched back to Heston as the entire Michigan team swept right. Heston took one step with them, then reversed and raced wide to the left, all by himself. He went 40 yards before he was forced out of bounds.

The Michigan team rode this horse-drawn "float" in the 1902 floral parade.

It was football's first bootleg play, and it gave the Wolverines the spark they needed. Willie Heston was a freshman and almost completely unknown at this point. Within a couple of years he would be the most feared running back in America.

A moment later Neil Snow cracked over center for the first touchdown. Then, while Stanford spent the rest of the game trying to stop Heston, Snow scored four more times in a stunning rout of the bewildered and heat-wilted Stanford team.

With six minutes still remaining, Michigan had already racked up 1,463 yards from scrimmage and was leading 49–0. Then the Stanford captain admitted that his team was exhausted. If Michigan would be willing to cut the game short it was okay with him.

The Wolverines, who had played the entire game in the 90-degree heat without a single substitution, agreed. The first Rose Bowl game was history—and it was the only one played in less than regulation time.

The Michigan team made the long journey home across the continent by train. Snow, who had scored five touchdowns, was more excited at the chance to see real, live Indians on the way back than he was over his great football performance.

Years later Michigan would play Stanford again in the Bowl. The trip would take four hours by jet, and the game would be seen by 100,000 fans at the stadium and millions of television viewers. In 1902 airplanes and television were still far off—but thanks to Pasadena, the Rose Bowl had arrived.

During the game, fans sat in stands on the far side of the field or stood on the sidelines.

2

A "World Series"

In 1903 several events hinted at the future. President Teddy Roosevelt sent the first round-the-world cable message, which was returned to him in twelve minutes. Modern communications were beginning to shrink the world. Transportation was changing, too. In 1903 a snorting Packard battled its way from San Francisco to New York in 52 days, completing the first transcontinental auto

trip. And in December the Wright brothers made man's first airplane flight (remaining aloft all of twelve seconds!). The first movie with a plot was made in Fort Lee, New Jersey. It was a "Western" called "The Great Train Robbery."

Sports, too, had a significant first. On October 1, the Boston Red Stockings and the Pittsburgh Pirates met in the first World

Series. It wasn't an altogether pleasant meeting. Baseball had been in serious trouble, and the new championship series was a step taken reluctantly to help save it.

Before 1900 pro baseball had been controlled by the National Baseball Federation (later the National League), the only so-called major league in existence. Baseball players were a rowdy crew. They drank, gambled and brawled off the field, and threatened umpires on the field. In turn, they were manhandled by the team owners, who rigidly controlled salaries, blackballed players, plotted against each other illegally to sign players and (some claimed) conspired to fix games. Baseball was a mess.

But in 1901 Ban Johnson, an ex-sports editor from Cincinnati, and Charles Comiskey, a former minor league player-manager, put together a new loop called The American League. They raided the established National for stars and drew up tough, sensible rules of player and owner conduct. The American League soon convinced the public that it was here to stay. With public approval, it claimed "major league" status and forced the National League to recognize its existence.

By 1903 the American League felt it had gained equality—its teams had lured many stars away from the National League—including Cy Young, the greatest pitcher of the era. During the 1903 season Young won 28 games and led the Boston Red Sox to the American League pennant. The Boston owner then challenged the National League winners, the Pittsburgh Pirates, to a world championship series.

Although the new league now had almost as many real stars as the National, the senior league sneeringly insisted that the American Leaguers played an inferior brand of ball. The National League didn't want to recognize the Americans by playing them. But with the fans now solidly on the side of the American League, Pittsburgh finally agreed to a best-of-nine series.

The Pirates were led by the great Honus Wagner, who had led the National League with a .355 batting average during the season. The honor of the league was at stake, and the Pirates vowed to end the series in five straight games.

On October 1, the Red Sox fans who jammed the wooden grandstands in Boston had little to cheer about. The Pirates scored four runs in the first inning against the great Cy Young. Pirate pitching ace Deacon Phillippe held the Red Sox, striking out ten, and the Pirates coasted to a 7–3 win.

In the second game Bill Dineen pitched for Boston. He shut out the powerful Pirates as Boston won 3–0, tying the series at one game apiece. But the next day Pittsburgh's Deacon Phillippe came back to whip the Red Sox 4–2 on a four-hitter.

When the series moved to Pittsburgh, the home team had a two-games-to-one lead. After one travel day and a day of rain, Pirate pitcher Phillippe pitched his third game. He went into the ninth inning with a

The great Cy Young pitched for Cleveland and St. Louis before going to Boston in 1903.

5–1 lead. The Red Sox put on a rally to score three runs, but Phillippe held on for a 5–4 victory. Now the superiority of the National League was starting to look like more than just a boast. The American League pipsqueaks were behind three games to one. Fans around the nation, who flocked to newspaper offices to get the latest scores from telegraph reports, were frankly disappointed.

Boston's only hope was that Cy Young could apply the stopper. He had already lost one game, and if he lost again he would become the goat of the series. But Young and the Boston batters shocked the Pirates. After five scoreless innings in the fourth game, the

Handsome Deacon Phillippe started five games for the Pirates, but could win only three.

Red Sox exploded for six runs in the sixth and four more in the seventh, going on to win 11–2.

The Red Sox were still alive. But there were still two more games to be played in Pittsburgh, and the Pirates only needed two games to win the series. The Red Sox called on Bill Dineen to keep their hopes up. With the help of a Pirate error, the Sox scored early and went on to win 6–3. The series was tied at three games apiece.

Another date was rained out. Then Cy Young faced Deacon Phillippe, who had pitched all three of the Pirates' victories. This would be the last game in Pittsburgh, and the fans overflowed the stadium. Hundreds stood in the outfield beyond the fielders, and a special ground rule provided that a ball going into the crowd was a triple. Phillippe had gotten plenty of rest, but this day he couldn't keep the Red Sox down. They got five of the ground-rule triples and won 7–3.

Suddenly it dawned on the nation's fans that the underdog Red Sox, coming back from a 3–1 deficit, now led the series four games to three. As the series returned to Boston, they needed only one more game to win the championship.

A travel day and another rainy day delayed the eighth game until Tuesday, October 13. Bill Dineen was picked to pitch by Boston's playing manager Fred Clarke. Dineen had won two games and lost one. His opponent? Deacon Phillippe, starting his fifth series game! But Phillippe couldn't hold the Red Sox. Boston second baseman Hobe Ferris drove in all three Red Sox runs, while Dineen shut out the Pirates on four hits. The upstart Red Sox had become baseball's first World Champions.

The underdog had won, providing an exciting start for the new series. A dispute between the leagues kept the series from being played in 1904, but it began again in 1905 and has been America's greatest annual sporting event ever since.

Bill Dineen, the Boston hero, never appeared in another World Series as a player, but as an umpire he later called the balls and strikes at seven of the fall classics. Cy Young never pitched in a World Series again, but he continued his mastery over the American League. By the time he retired in 1911, he had won 510 games. No other pitcher would ever come close to Young's record.

As for the Pirates, they would return to the World Series after a few years away. In 1909, still led by the amazing Honus Wagner, they would meet the Detroit Tigers and another amazing player named Ty Cobb.

The new league had given baseball a much-needed boost—but now football was in jeopardy.

3

Point-a-Minute Football

The big story in football continued to be "Hurry-Up" Yost's University of Michigan team. After defeating Stanford in the first Rose Bowl game, the Michigan Wolverines went on to three undefeated seasons, rolling up even more points than their 1901 total of 550.

In 1902 they scored 644 to their opponents' 12.

In 1903 it was 565 to 6.

And in 1904 it was 567 to 22.

Michigan's leading star had been Willie Heston, the great back who had set up the first touchdown against Stanford in the Rose Bowl. Carrying the ball in those early days was tough work. Since the forward pass was illegal, defenses lined up with a nine-man line. To offset the tremendous rush of nine players, the offensive men would form a human wedge behind the line of scrimmage, sometimes even locking arms, to escort the runner through the defense. Players wore little or no padding and no helmets, so injuries were common. Slugging, kicking and kneeing were also common, and sometimes officials lost control of the game. So Willie Heston, who scored more than 100 touchdowns, could be credited not only with skill but with plenty of courage.

Heston graduated in June 1905, so Michigan began the 1905 season without its top star. But as the season progressed, it became

clear that Michigan could do almost as well without him. On Thanksgiving Day, as the Wolverines faced their last opponent of the season, they had won every game, scoring 495 points and allowing none. They had not been defeated in 55 games (a 6–6 tie with Minnesota in 1903 was the only game they hadn't won). Now they were playing the University of Chicago, coached by Amos Alonzo Stagg. Stagg had been director of

The legendary "Hurry-Up" Yost, who coached football's most overpowering team.

Little Walter Eckersall, star of the University of Chicago Maroons in 1905.

athletics and a coach at Chicago since the university opened in 1892, and he knew a thing or two about football. In 1904 his team had scored twelve points against Michigan—the best any opponent had done in four years—but had lost anyway. In 1905 the Chicago Maroons were unbeaten going into the Michigan game, so spectators expected Chicago to provide the Wolverines with their sternest test of the season. But what is a stern test to a team that has outscored its opponents 495–0? Stagg's Chicago team might provide some excitement, but they would never win.

Chicago's biggest hope was their smallest player, a 140-pound back named Walter Eckersall. In a day when every player played both offense and defense, little Eckie did everything well. He could run—clocking a 100-yard dash in 9.8 seconds (then nearly world-record time). When passing became legal in his senior year in 1906, he threw his first pass ever for a 75-yard touchdown. Since field goals were worth five points and

the sluggish running offenses of the day were often stopped dead, kicking was an essential part of the game. And Eckie was the greatest kicker of the era. Finally, he was a tenacious safety man on defense, often tackling men nearly twice his size.

More than 20,000 people were in the Chicago Stadium to cheer on the Maroon as they faced the legendary Michigan team. The game turned into a titanic defensive battle. Halfway through the fourth quarter neither team had scored. Then Michigan got the ball and drove deep into Chicago territory. The Maroon put up a heroic fight and stopped Michigan on the 2-yard-line, taking possession of the ball.

Chicago, backed up against its own goal line, had three downs to make five yards according to the rules of the day. After two plays, they were short of a first down, so Eckersall dropped back into his own end zone to punt the ball out. Eckie saw that the Michigan ends on the nine-man line were playing tight in order to knife in and block the kick. He knew what he'd do. He took the snap, circled swiftly to his right, between the goal posts, and headed upfield with the ball. He stumbled at the 50 and was pushed out of bounds.

Again the Michigan line halted Chicago, so Eckie went back to punt once more. This time he got off a towering kick that was caught by Michigan's Denny Clark, in his own end zone. Clark decided to run it out, thinking he could catch Chicago napping and go all the way. But just as he reached the goal line he was hit low by a lineman and hit high by Chicago's All-America end, Mark Catlin. Clark landed behind the goal line. It was a safety. Chicago fans cheered wildly as the 2–0 score went up on the board.

The slim lead almost didn't hold up. A Michigan ball carrier, cracking through the line, bore down on Eckie, the safetyman. Eckie dove, and the Wolverine hurdled over his flying body. Eckie did a complete flip-flop with his body and wound up on his feet.

The flying wedge formation, in which the ballcarrier was surrounded by blockers . . .

Instantly, he took off after the Michigan back and dragged him down on the Chicago 20-yard-line.

Minutes later Michigan's amazing unbeaten streak was ended at 55, by the margin of a safety. There would be other long unbeaten streaks in football, but no major team would ever match that of the legendary "Point-a-Minute" team.

But even with all its excitement, football was in deep trouble. After the season, Northwestern would announce that it was dropping the sport. And the president of the University of Michigan showed grave concern over the future of the game. He complained that football had assumed too much importance on university campuses and that it was too expensive.

. . . caused injuries like the one shown in this 1891 engraving.

But the major complaint was that football had become too dangerous. Each year 15 or 20 players died of injuries, and dozens more were permanently maimed. One editorial writer described football as "wasteful, wanton barbarity . . . not fit for humans to indulge in, or even witness."

Changes were needed, but who would take the first step? The initiative came from an unexpected observer—Theodore Roosevelt, the President of the United States. Roosevelt had been an ardent sportsman, so he was no foe of athletics. But he, too, was concerned about the weekly reports of death and injury.

A few weeks before the Michigan–Chicago game, newspapers had reported three football deaths in one weekend. That was enough for Teddy Roosevelt. If the football rulesmakers wouldn't act, he would. Although he had no real power to change the game (some said he had no business interfering), he summoned representatives of Harvard, Yale and Princeton (football's traditional Big Three) to the White House.

So, late in November of 1905, the university men visited the President. They were startled when he began to complain about football. He pounded his desk, his mustache bristling angrily. He told them that if something wasn't done about football's brutish aspects, he would abolish the sport. They stared in disbelief.

Could a president interfere with private sports in the United States? Probably not. But this was no ordinary president, and his influence could be immense. Get rid of mass play by opening up the game, he told them. Do anything necessary to see that the game could be played safely. So, on January 12, 1906, shaken by Roosevelt's order, college football formed a rules body which was the forerunner of the National Collegiate Athletic Association (NCAA). And it immediately made changes that saved football. First, it legalized the forward pass with certain limitations. This was bound to open up the game. New rules also required the offense to make ten yards (instead of five) in three tries for a first down. This would force the offense to use more wide sweeps and other open plays. (Later, it was changed to ten yards in four tries.) To further discourage mass play, six offensive men were required to be on the line of scrimmage when the ball was snapped, to prevent linemen from serving as mass momentum interference. Penalties for roughing were put in.

All of a sudden, football began to lose its brutish character. And all because a United States president decided to run some interference of his own.

4

Ty Cobb Steals Home

In 1908 William Howard Taft was elected president. During his term of office he became the first chief executive to throw out the first ball of the major league season. It was a big event, if only because Taft was America's biggest president, weighing in at nearly 350 pounds.

The biggest man in baseball during Taft's presidency weighed only 178 pounds, but he was a pure concentrate of athletic ability and competitive fury. In 1909 Tyrus Raymond Cobb was only 22, but he was in his fourth full season with the Detroit Tigers.

Cobb first appeared with the Tigers on August 30, 1905. To those who know what Cobb went on to achieve, his first time at bat in the majors qualifies as one of the great moments in the game. But to the fans

An intense, scowling Ty Cobb waits for the pitch in one of his early games with Detroit.

in Detroit's Bennett Field that day, Cobb was just a raw 18-year-old coming up to face Jack Chesbro, the ace pitcher of the New York Highlanders (later called the Yankees).

Two men were on for the Tigers. Chesbro looked confidently down at the hitter. Cobb was grim, scowling back. Chesbro smiled. Cobb shouted some nasty words toward the mound. *Bush-league kid!,* Chesbro thought.

Then he pumped and threw. Ty Cobb lashed out with his bat and drilled a screaming double to right field, driving in two runs.

When Chesbro turned to look at the kid standing on second, the kid glared at him. Getting a hit had not lessened his intensity —the kind of intensity that American League players would soon come to fear.

That was just the beginning for Cobb. In 1909 he won baseball's Triple Crown with a .377 average, 9 home runs and 107 runs batted in. It was the third straight year Cobb had won the American League batting championship and the third straight year the Tigers had won the pennant.

Unfortunately, although the Tigers seemed to have no trouble winning pennants, the World Series was another matter. In the past two years they had lost the Series 4–0 and 4–1 to the Chicago Cubs. But at the end of the 1909 season they faced a different team—the Pittsburgh Pirates, the team that had lost the first World Series back in 1903. The Pirates had a hero of their own: their shortstop Honus Wagner had led the National League in batting three seasons in a row. At 35 years of age, Wagner was considered the greatest all-around player in the game.

The Pirates were favored in the Series, and they won the first game easily. Then in the first inning of the second game they scored two runs to take the lead. The Tigers, determined not to be routed in a Series once again, tallied two in the second to tie the score. In the third inning, the Tigers threatened again. With two out, they had runners at second and third. The runner at third was young Ty Cobb, who was about to demonstrate one of the skills that would help him replace Honus Wagner as baseball's biggest star.

In this sticky situation, the Pirates brought in a relief pitcher, Vic Willis. That gave Cobb his chance. "The minute I saw Willis was going in," Cobb later wrote, "I decided I'd try to steal home. I calculated that Willis,

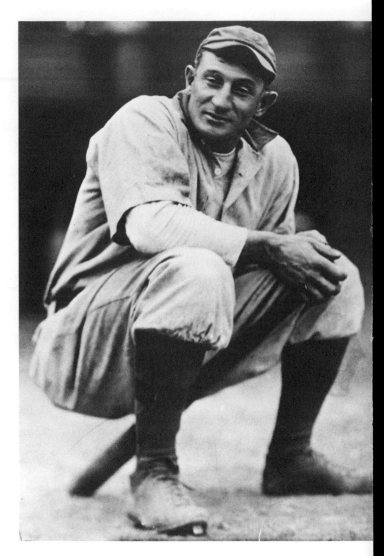

Honus Wagner of Pittsburgh was the greatest player of the decade . . .

coming in at such a time, would give no thought to me at third—that his mind would be entirely on the batter. . . .

"So when he got on the rubber I walked some distance off third base to see if he was paying me any attention. I observed he was looking at his catcher. I turned back toward third to disarm the third baseman and the catcher. Then, just as Willis raised his arm in his preliminary motion, I dashed for the plate.

"As there was a right-handed batter up, I had some protection, and in sliding I threw my body away from the plate, giving the catcher only my foot to touch in case he got the ball in time. I ripped the ground about thirty inches with my spikes before I touched the rubber, but I made it all right."

Cheered by Cobb's spectacular daring, the Tigers scored two more runs that inning and went on to win the game. They ultimately lost the Series in the seventh game, but that one play by Cobb—stealing home—was the talk of the Series. Honus Wagner had driven in seven runs and stolen six bases to maintain his claim as the greatest, but Cobb was already erasing that claim with his bat, his gloves and his spikes.

After 1909 Cobb never played on another pennant-winning team. But whether his club was good or bad, whether they were winning or losing, Cobb never let up. He became a legend as a ferocious base-runner, sliding into base with his spikes high. In 1915 he stole 96 bases, a record that would hold for 47 years. Three times he hit over .400 for a full season, and he was the league's leading batter twelve times.

By the time he retired in 1928 at the age of 41, Cobb's records filled the book. He had played in the most games (3,034), gotten the most hits (4,192), scored the most runs (2,245), stolen the most bases (892) and maintained the highest lifetime average (.367).

Thirty years after Cobb stole home in the World Series, the Baseball Hall of Fame opened its doors at Cooperstown, New York. It was fitting that the first thing displayed there was a pair of Ty Cobb's gleaming spiked shoes.

. . . but Ty Cobb, shown here in a posed sliding shot, would become the greatest ever.

PART II
1910-1919

As America entered the second decade of the century, women were demonstrating for the right to vote. Cars—especially Henry Ford's Model T—were becoming a common sight, and roads near major cities were beginning to be paved. The territories of Arizona and New Mexico were preparing to become states—the last of the "old 48." There would be no more states created for more than 40 years.

The country was still a nation of immigrants, and the years 1910 to 1919 brought the last great wave of the foreign-born. Their sons and daughters would add luster to the American scene for years to come, and in sports some of their names would become legend—Nagurski, Lombardi, Greenberg, Rizzuto, Marciano, Luisetti, Unitas, Namath, Csonka, Butkus.

In August 1914 the countries of Europe went to war. Most Americans believed that the United States should stay out of the conflict, but as the battles raged through 1915 and 1916, it became clear that staying out would be impossible. In April 1917 President Woodrow Wilson asked Congress for a declaration of war, and the country was rapidly mobilized. Hundreds of thousands of young men were eventually sent to France to fight for the Allied powers.

The war, which would come to be known as World War I, ended in November 1918. The strain of the war effort and the division of the nation over President Wilson's proposals for the peace settlement caused the decade to

end on a sour note. The war had interrupted American life, and citizens were eager to return to home concerns.

For sports, the decade was one of growth. In 1911 the Indianapolis 500 established a new sports tradition. The next year a strong American team competed in the Olympic Games at Stockholm, Sweden. Baseball was dominated by the Philadelphia Athletics managed by Connie Mack and the New York Giants led by John McGraw. And in 1916 a young pitcher named Babe Ruth led the Boston Red Sox to the pennant and a World Series triumph.

College football continued to spread across the country, and some current football powers fielded their first great teams—Notre Dame, Ohio State, Oklahoma and Nebraska. Meanwhile, in the industrial cities of Pennsylvania, leagues of professional players were being organized. The personality of the era was Indian Jim Thorpe, who lent his amazing talents to college and pro football, Olympic track and field and major league baseball. From 1910 to 1916 the world heavyweight boxing crown was held by Jack Johnson, the first black champion. Meanwhile, a young heavyweight named Jack Dempsey was making his reputation in the rough mining towns of the West.

The World War slowed sports down as fans turned to more serious concerns. But as the 1920s approached, American sport was on the threshold of its golden era. Many of the athletes who first appeared in the teens would make the '20s a time to remember.

500 Miles at Indy

At five o'clock in the morning on May 30, 1911, security officers fanned out over the grounds of the Indianapolis Motor Speedway. They were looking for the gate-crashers who hid under the bleachers or roosted in tall trees, trying to beat the $1.00 general admission charge. About 200 early-birds were finally rousted out.

At 6:30 A.M. an aerial bomb exploded overhead, and all gates were opened for what would be a history-making event—the first annual Indianapolis 500-Mile Race. Spectators came by shuttle train from Midwestern cities, by trolley car and by horse and buggy. More than 3,000 hitching posts were provided for the horses.

An early poster for the Speedway.

Soon there were 80,000 people in the stands waiting to see 40 racing cars roar around a brick track for 500 miles. It was the largest crowd ever assembled for a sports event in America. No one would have believed or predicted such interest—no one but a man named Carl G. Fisher.

In the early years of the 20th century people were quickly convinced that the automobile, noisy and crude as it was, was here to stay. Clattering along the newly paved roads were automobiles with names like Peerless, Stutz, Winton, Stanley Steamer, Chadwick, Napier, Overland and Ford. The self-starter had just been invented, and now for the first time a woman could drive alone without a male companion to crank the engine back to life if it stalled.

But even before most people dreamed of owning one, the automobile had also spawned a new sport. By 1905 auto races were being held—mostly on dirt roads or on beaches. Fisher, a young Indianapolis manufacturer, convinced some friends that a huge oval track would help establish auto racing as a major sport. He also felt such a track would be an ideal testing laboratory for motors, brakes, tires and other auto equipment.

In the fall of 1908 Fisher and his group began to build their speedway on a 400-acre field in Indianapolis. Hundreds of men worked for $2.00 a day on the 2.5-mile dirt oval, using mules to do the heavy lifting and hauling. At first the track was used only for sprint races. But Fisher was dreaming of a longer, more dramatic race—perhaps 500 miles, or 200 times around the oval.

But the early sprint races had proved that a dirt track wouldn't do for a long race. After a while, clouds of dust would obscure the view and choke the drivers. So Fisher made a bold decision: he would pave the whole track with bricks. In one year workmen laid 3,200,000 bricks weighing ten pounds each, over the huge oval's dirt surface.

Then Fisher scheduled his first race, to be held on Memorial Day 1911. The best cars and drivers from all over the world were invited to compete for a fortune in prize money—$35,000. If all went well, Fisher thought, the big race might attract 40,000 people.

The 80,000 who actually poured through the gates had come to see cars that might reach the incredible speed of 100 miles per hour on the straightaways. But how long could these primitive cars last? Would any of them survive 500 miles of brick pavement? What the 80,000 saw was drama, tragedy and thrills—the kind that would insure tremendous success for the Indy 500.

Forty cars were bunched behind the starting line, awaiting the signal for the race. In road races, cars were strung out for miles, with each car's time kept separately. But at the new Speedway they would start from the same point and roar around the same course for 500 miles.

Of the 40 cars, 39 had two passengers— a driver and a mechanic. It was the mechanic's job to let the driver know when another racer was coming up behind him to pass. He also listened for ominous engine noises.

But one car carried only a single passenger—Ray Harroun, an engineer for the Marmon Motor Car Company. He had been a race driver but had quit racing the year before. Now he was back for the 500 because Marmon had modified its little Marmon Wasp, and thought it would have a good chance to win the huge purse.

Harroun got in trouble when he announced that he would drive the Marmon all by himself. The day before the race, other drivers protested. They said that if Harroun raced without a mechanic to let him know when another car was trying to pass, the other cars and drivers would be endangered. Still, Harroun refused to carry a mechanic. But to answer the other drivers' objections, he spent hours fitting a rectangular piece of mirror with a metal frame to his cowling. He had pioneered the use of the first rear-view mirror, and the other drivers reluctantly agreed to let him race.

Another aerial bomb signaled the drivers

Cars roar down the dusty track in the first Indianapolis 500.

to start their engines. When all 40 cars started their motors at the same time, spectators had to cover their ears against the roar. Great clouds of black smoke belched from the racers' exhausts. The strong odor of benzene and castor oil swept over the stands. It was indeed an awesome event, never witnessed before.

In starting formation the cars followed the pace car around the track. Then the starting flag flashed down.

On the twelfth lap a driver named Art Greiner lost control of his Simplex and slammed into a wall. His riding mechanic, Sam Dickson, was killed. Dickson was the first to lose his life in the deadly 500. There would be many more.

After 40 laps there was an epidemic of blowouts, and car after car made pit stops for new tires.

On lap 87 came the kind of drama that would be the hallmark of the Indy 500. Mechanic C. L. Anderson leaned too far over the side of Joe Jagersberger's car, a Case, and tumbled onto the track. The crowd screamed in horror. Harry Knight, trailing, swung his Wescott desperately to avoid the sprawled Anderson. He missed him only by lurching into the pit area, where he smashed into another car in a dreadful pile-up.

Ralph DePalma, Ralph Mulford, David Bruce-Brown and Art Chevrolet were running ahead at the 150-mile mark. Many fans were hardly aware of the yellow and black bullet-shaped Marmon that had begun to pass car after car. Soon it was in fifth place, then fourth, then third.

By then the track was slippery with oil. Workmen desperately shoveled sand on the slick surface, but it didn't help much. In a few years engineers would conquer some of the oil dripping problem, but now only a miracle would keep the track from becoming a killer.

Nearing the end, tire changes were needed by Harroun in his Marmon Wasp and Mulford in his Lozier, but it had settled down to a three-car race between the Wasp, the Lozier and the Fiat of Englishman David Bruce-Brown. With just a few laps to go, the Fiat quit with ignition trouble. Ray Harroun roared past Mulford into first place and held on. Six hours and 42 minutes after the race began, Harroun roared past the finish line, winning the first Indy 500 with an average speed of 74.59 miles per hour. And he had done it all by himself. Sixty years later, drivers would cover the 500 miles in less than half the time, averaging more than 150 miles per hour. But for the huge crowd at Indy in 1911, Harroun's speed and endurance were amazing. Like the automobile itself, the noise and speed and excitement of auto racing were here to stay.

Roy Harroun streaks down the home stretch to win the race, his rear-view mirror perched in front of the steering wheel.

The World's Greatest Athlete

One day in the summer of 1912 the ocean liner *Finland* pulled out of New York Harbor. On board were members of the United States Olympic team, who were on their way to the Olympic Games in Stockholm, Sweden. The trip to Stockholm would take eleven days, so the ship was filled with training equipment to help the athletes work out and stay in condition. But one of the team members never worked out. While others jogged around the cork track on the deck, lifted weights and did calisthenics, he lay in his bunk or on a deck chair and dozed.

His name was Jim Thorpe. And within weeks he would be the most famous athlete in the world.

Thorpe was an American Indian of the Sac-Fox tribe. He was born in the Indian territories (later the state of Oklahoma) in 1888. At the age of 16 he went to the Carlisle Institute, a trade school for Indians in Pennsylvania. There he was to learn the trade of tailoring.

In 1907 Carlisle got a new football coach named Glenn "Pop" Warner. During Warner's first season, the 155-pound Thorpe was a substitute fullback. During a tough game against the University of Pennsylvania, Thorpe was sent in for the regular fullback and scored on a 65-yard run in his second play. The next time he got the ball he ran 85 yards for another touchdown. With Thorpe's help, little Carlisle crushed mighty Penn 26–6. It soon became clear that Thorpe was a great football player. Not only could he run, but he could kick the heavy, ungainly football 50 yards or more on punts or field goals. And he could pass as well. In 1908 he was named to the third team of Walter Camp's All-America.

In the spring Thorpe played baseball and

Jim Thorpe on the boat to Stockholm.

competed in track and field. It seemed that there was no athletic competition he couldn't win. He sprinted, he hurdled; he broad-jumped and high-jumped; he threw the discus and the javelin. And he could hit the baseball a mile.

But at the end of school in 1909, Thorpe left Carlisle. That summer he played semi-professional baseball in the South. Then he went home to the reservation in Oklahoma.

Pop Warner finally talked Thorpe into coming back to Carlisle in 1911. He was now 23 years old, stood 6-foot-1 and weighed 188 pounds. And he was still eligible for football. During the fall of 1911 Thorpe became famous—to football fans. The Carlisle Indians were undefeated, and in their biggest game of the year Thorpe almost single-handedly defeated a Harvard team that had been picked to win the national championship. He kicked three field goals and carried the ball nine straight times to score the tying touchdown. Then he kicked a 50-yard field goal to win the game 18–15. This time he was named to Camp's first-team All-America.

In the spring of 1912 Thorpe's track ability came into full flower. In a meet against Lafayette College, the Indians of Carlisle brought only four athletes. One won the mile run and the two-mile run. A second won the 440-yard dash and the 880-yard dash. A third won the hammer throw. Jim Thorpe took third in the 100-yard dash. Then he won the high jump, long jump, shot put, discus, high hurdles and low hurdles. Carlisle won 71–41.

Soon afterward Thorpe qualified for the Olympic team and left for Stockholm. There he would compete in the decathlon, the greatest test of all-round athletic ability ever invented—ten events over two days. On the first day he would compete in the 100-meter dash, the long jump, the shot put, the high jump and the 400-meter dash. On the second day he would try the 110-meter high hurdles, the pole vault, the javelin throw, the discus throw and finally the 1,500-meter run. The decathlon was scheduled to be the climax of Olympic competition, and those who trained for it trained for nothing else.

Almost as an afterthought, Thorpe decided to enter the pentathlon, a separate

Thorpe is said to have drop-kicked a field goal of 75 yards.

competition of five events in one day. The pentathlon was to be held only three days before the decathlon. How could Thorpe do both, especially if he refused to train?

As the *Finland* approached Stockholm, Thorpe remained in his bunk. The first few days in Sweden he worked out lightly. Then he discovered a hammock and spent most of his days napping in it, waiting for his events. The American track coach, a stern disciplinarian, was outraged. But Pop Warner was there, and he maintained that Thorpe would do everything expected of him in competition even if he wasn't too good at training.

Today the Olympics have an event called the modern pentathlon, consisting of five

Jim throws the javelin on his way to pentathlon and decathlon gold medals at Stockholm.

"modern" events: running, target shooting, swimming, fencing and horsemanship. But the pentathlon that Jim Thorpe entered was all track and field: a 200-meter dash, javelin throw, long jump, discus throw and 1,500-meter run. Thorpe finished third in the javelin throw—but he placed first in all four of the other events. He won his first gold medal easily.

Then, with only two days of rest, Thorpe was ready for the sports world's most demanding event. His performance in the pentathlon had made him a favorite in the decathlon, but many wondered if he would be fresh enough to win.

On the first day of competition he placed well in the first two events, then won the shot put and the high jump and placed well in the 400-meter dash. He started the second day by winning the high hurdles. Although he didn't win any of the next three events, he was well ahead of the other contestants on total points. Then in the final event, the grueling 1,500-meter run, Thorpe was able

to win even though distance running had never been his strong point.

All in all, it was a stunning performance. Thorpe had won four of the ten events, and he finished far ahead of the field. His days of resting on the boat and in Stockholm must have paid off. On the victory stand, Thorpe received his second gold medal from the King of Sweden. "You, sir, are the greatest athlete in the world!" the King said warmly.

The whole world agreed with the King. Jim Thorpe went home to a huge welcoming parade in New York. President Taft sent his congratulations. Vaudeville producers offered Jim $1,500 a week to tour the country, but he turned them down. He went back to Carlisle to be football captain in his last year of play.

Every Carlisle opponent wished that Thorpe had accepted the vaudeville offers. In a game against Army he returned a punt 90 yards for a touchdown. When the play was called back on a penalty, Thorpe took the next punt and ran it back 95 yards. With

25 touchdowns for the season, Thorpe was a unanimous All-America.

But Jim Thorpe's story had an unhappy ending. That winter a sportswriter reported that Thorpe had received money for playing semi-professional baseball in the summer of 1910. If the report was true, Thorpe would lose his status as an amateur and had been ineligible for the Olympics.

When the Amateur Athletic Union (AAU) asked Thorpe about the charge, he admitted it. "I was just a simple Indian boy," he said. "I wasn't wise in the ways of the world. The other college players used different names, but I didn't think anything of it. I hope you can overlook this on my part."

But the AAU took an iron-firm stand on the rules and ordered Thorpe to return his two gold medals. The heartbroken young athlete did as he was told, and the medals were offered to the second-place finishers in each event. The second man in the decathlon is said to have refused the medal, saying, "Thorpe won it—not I." Thousands of fans in America and around the world agreed.

7

Passing for Notre Dame

In 1913 the people of the United States were sent into shock by the 16th Amendment to the Constitution, a shock from which they would never recover. The 16th Amendment established Federal income taxes, which have been levied every year from then to now.

The game of football also received a shock that would permanently change the game. Although the forward pass had been legal for several years, the most successful teams, especially those in the East, still hesitated to use it much.

One reason for their reluctance was that the technique of throwing and catching the ball was still being perfected. Passers had to learn how to throw the ball (which was less streamlined than the modern ball) so that it would not tumble end over end. Early receivers ran out to a prearranged spot, then turned around and waited for the ball, cradling it in their arms when it came.

Another problem was that the coaches considered the pass too risky. An incomplete pass was a play lost and an interception was a disaster.

Still, the more daring teams began to find in the forward pass a weapon that could win a game in one play. Long before 1913, passing was common outside the East. But the established football powers still scorned it, preferring to rely on a precision ground game.

The pass finally came to the East in one of the most amazing games in football history. On November 1, 1913, the Army was scheduled to play little-known Notre Dame on its home field at West Point, New York. The sportswriters who came out to see the game weren't very interested in Notre Dame. They were there to see an Army team that was hoping to win a national championship. Army thought its difficult games were still ahead on the schedule and welcomed a chance to warm up against the little school from Indiana.

The previous summer, two young Notre Dame players—quarterback Gus Dorais and end Knute Rockne—had taken jobs at the same summer resort on the shores of Lake Erie. They brought a football with them, and day after day they practiced as a passing combination. Dorais was a fine thrower, and Rockne had some new ideas

The first great receiver, Knute Rockne, takes a solemn pose for the camera.

on receiving a football. He wondered why a receiver had to make a basket catch, so he tried catching the ball with his hands while on the run. Dorais threw over Rockne's head, at his feet, to his left and to his right, and soon the Norwegian immigrant could catch almost anything. This passing combination helped Notre Dame win three crushing victories early in the 1913 season over small Midwestern opponents. But of course Army knew nothing about that.

The lighter Notre Dame team held the Army through most of the first quarter, but quarterback Dorais kept the ball on the ground and neither team scored. Then late in the period he threw three straight completions to his halfback Joe Pliska. On each play Rockne just loped downfield. On the next passing play Rockne cruised downfield again, then suddenly took off at full speed. The Army defenders were caught flat-footed. Rockne caught Dorais' pass over one shoulder and raced across the goal.

Army came back to score two touchdowns and go ahead 13–7. But then Rockne got loose again, catching a 35-yard pass at the 5-yard-line. When he came back to the huddle he was grinning. "This is going to be a picnic," he said. "They just don't understand how to defend against the pass."

He was right. The Irish mixed their running and passing plays. Rockne ran through and around the Army defense, threatening to catch the ball even when he didn't actually do it. Dorais threw all kinds of passes—short ones over the middle, long ones to either side, to several different receivers. The unheralded Notre Dame squad just ran away from Army, winning 35–13.

Dorais completed 17 of 24 passes, ten of them to Rockne. When the game was over, shocked Eastern sportswriters reported that the forward pass had arrived. Gus Dorais was voted All-America quarterback at the end of the season, the first passing quarterback ever to win. Football had entered its modern age.

8

Heavyweight Massacre

In 1917 and 1918 the United States was at war. Millions of young men, including most athletes, volunteered or were drafted for military service, and the people at home turned their attention to the war effort. The U.S. troops helped the Allies defeat the Central Powers, and many believed that this "war to end wars" would bring lasting peace. Fighting ended in November 1918, and the following month President Woodrow Wilson sailed to France to participate in the Peace Conference. American boys returned, and the nation was relieved to turn its attention once more to home interests—including sports.

The first major post-war event was a heavyweight championship fight. July 4, 1919, was a steaming hot day in Toledo, Ohio, and interest in the two fighters was nearly as warm. The defending champion was gigantic Jess Willard, who stood 6-foot-6 and weighed 260 pounds. In 1916 he had won the championship from Jack Johnson, the first black champ, in a controversial fight at Havana, Cuba. Many claimed that Johnson had thrown the fight in a gambling fix, but many others thought that Willard, a former Kansas farm boy, was truly the greatest fighter in the world.

Now Willard was being challenged by a 24-year-old tough from the gold-mining town of Manassa, Colorado. At 6-foot-1 and 182 pounds, the challenger looked like a pygmy beside the giant Willard. Some fans despised him because he had not volunteered for service during the war. But most people agreed he was a fine boxer. In the 18 months before Toledo he had knocked out 27 men in 27 fights. He was lithe and quick as a tiger, and in the ring he had the instincts of a killer. His name was Jack Dempsey.

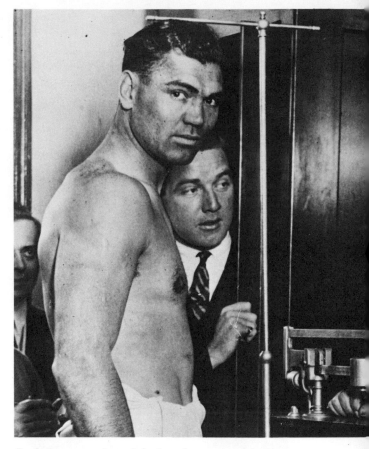

Jack Dempsey is weighed and measured before a championship fight.

Jess Willard was contemptuous of Dempsey, however. His manager had demanded $100,000 for the fight, and Willard boasted that it would be the easiest money he would ever earn. Just before the fight he predicted, "Dempsey will come rushing right at me. I'll stick out my left. He'll run into it. Then I'll come in with a right uppercut, and it'll be all over in the first round."

Some ringsiders agreed with that prediction. Dempsey might be a tiger, but even a tiger couldn't cope with an elephant.

In round one, Dempsey circled the champ

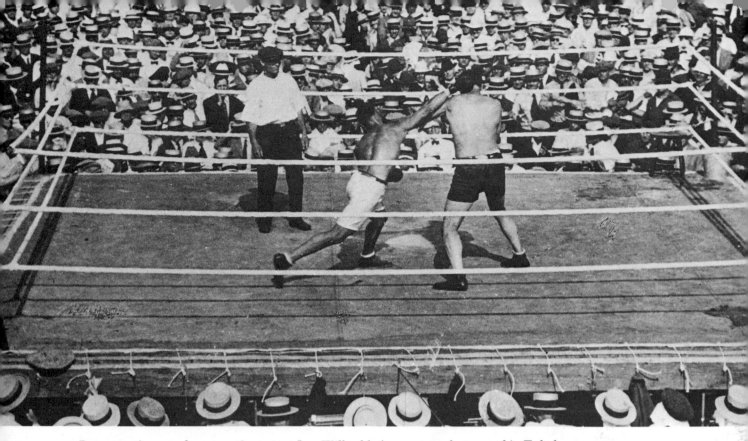

Dempsey throws a long punch at giant Jess Willard before a straw-hat crowd in Toledo.

for half a minute. The challenger's hair was clipped like a brush on top, and his face seemed set in a scowl, his eyes narrowed under thick, black brows. Dempsey looked like a man who meant business. But the confident Willard, towering over his opponent, didn't seem to notice.

Dempsey circled for a few seconds more. Willard finally grew impatient. He moved in on Dempsey and threw a left at Dempsey's head. Ringsiders barely saw what happened next.

Dempsey ducked like a flash and rammed a savage right to the champ's middle. In a blur of motion he landed a left hook on the side of Willard's head. The champion went down. Within the next two minutes Willard went down five more times as the cat-like Dempsey swarmed over him with smashing combinations, thrown so fast that sportswriters couldn't even count them.

With seconds left in the first round, Willard was a bloody, helpless hulk. A sixth knockdown had left him hanging on the ropes. Amid the swelling roar of the crowd, the referee was raising Dempsey's hand in victory.

Quickly Dempsey ducked through the ropes and hurried down from the ring. He didn't get far. Suddenly people were pulling him back to the ring. The bell had rung, ending the round, and in the terrific din the referee hadn't heard it. Willard had not been officially knocked out, so the fight would go on.

No one had ever witnessed what went on in the second and third rounds. No heavyweight champion had ever taken such a beating from such a merciless pursuer. Jess Willard, as described by one writer, looked like ". . . an ox that was being butchered alive and on the hoof."

Between the third and fourth rounds, Willard lolled helplessly on his stool, head hanging, face bloody and swollen. When Jess Willard was unable to answer the bell for the fourth round, Jack Dempsey became the new heavyweight champion.

Boxing was still a disreputable sport— and Jack Dempsey seemed an unlikely candidate to make it more respectable. But the Golden '20s were just ahead, and within a few years a heavyweight championship would be the biggest event in all of sport.

PART III

1920-1929

In 1920 Warren G. Harding was elected President on the rallying cry, "Let us return to normalcy!" But as the post-war decade progressed, it became clear that times were even better than "normal." The United States was living through a zany, exciting and prosperous age that would someday be called "The Roaring Twenties."

Millions of people invested in the stock market for the first time, and the prices went up and up and up, promising even a working man the chance to get rich. The same working man might also be saving to buy a car. The automobile was no longer a novelty; it had become a mark of success and prestige.

Among adventurers, the style was fast cars and airplanes, which were slowly becoming a reliable form of transportation. The most exciting public event of the decade was the arrival in Paris of Charles Lindbergh, who had flown his single-engined *Spirit of St. Louis* across the Atlantic all by himself.

For less daring souls, the place to be was the movie house, where films alternated with live vaudeville entertainment—or the dance hall, where new dances like the Charleston were catching the imagination of the young. In 1927 the films got sound for the first time, and the "talkies" made movie-going more popular than ever.

Yet the '20s were also a time of moral fervor. As the decade began, Congress and the states ratified a constitutional amendment forbidding the sale of

Women crusaders celebrate winning the vote in 1920 . . . two charmers do the Charleston . . . and Charles Lindbergh poses in front of his Spirit of St. Louis.

alcoholic beverages. The great revivalist preacher Billy Sunday toured the country seeking to bring people back to God. And women, who had only received the right to vote in 1920, began crusading for more rights. Many were going to work in jobs that used to be reserved for men.

The popular heroes of the day were not politicians or generals. Instead, they were adventurers, entertainers, and especially athletes. For in a nation growing prosperous, there was spare time for sports and pastimes of a dozen different descriptions. Baseball maintained its place as the country's leading sport, with football following close behind. In the Northeast, hockey became a major sport, and the game of basketball, invented only 30 years before, was gaining attention. Huge stadiums and arenas went up all over the country, along with golf courses and tennis courts. When there were no regularly scheduled sporting events, promoters would dream up new games: six-day bicycle races, endurance swimming, even flagpole sitting and marathon dance contests.

Looking back, sportswriters would call the '20s "The Golden Age of Sports." The heroes of that decade seemed to stand out from those who preceded and those who followed. Their names and their accomplishments would be remembered and revered for many decades to come. And for the first time, some of the top sports stars would be women.

For a few brief years, sport was king. In less happy times, people would look back at its great moments and wistfully recall the "good old days."

9

The House That Ruth Built

Home run sensation Babe Ruth as he appeared in 1923, the year Yankee Stadium opened.

Not knowing that a golden age was approaching, sports fans in 1920 looked at the sports scene with a skeptical eye. In the fall of that year it had been revealed that the 1919 World Series between the Chicago White Sox and the Cincinnati Reds had been "fixed" by several White Sox players. The team promptly became known as the Black Sox, and after court hearings several of the players were banned from baseball for life.

Shoeless Joe Jackson, one of the great hitters in the history of the game, was one of the players involved in the scandal. After he confessed his part in the scheme, he was met on the steps of the courthouse by a young newsboy with tears in his eyes.

"Say it ain't so, Joe!" the boy pleaded. Yet sadly, it was so.

Disillusioned with baseball, the fans began wondering what other games might have been rigged to benefit gamblers. Fortunately, the man who would make them forget their doubts and believe in baseball again had already begun to revolutionize the game—and draw fans to ball parks in ever-increasing numbers. He was Babe Ruth.

Before 1920 Babe Ruth had established himself as one of the great pitchers in baseball, playing for the Boston Red Sox. But in 1918 and 1919 the Sox began using him as an outfielder on days when he wasn't pitching. He might be valuable as a pitcher, but he was almost unbelievable as a hitter. In 1919 he broke the all-time major league record by hitting 29 home runs. Baseball owners began to realize the appeal of the home run—and the men who hit them—so they voted to begin using a new, livelier ball in 1920.

By the time the 1920 season began, Babe Ruth had left Boston. Because the owners of the Boston team were in financial trouble, they had sold him for $125,000 to the New York Yankees, a lackluster team that had never won an American League pennant. The Yankees played in New York's Polo Grounds, sharing the huge old park with the far more successful New York Giants. They were hoping that Ruth would give them something different—perhaps even make them a winning team.

And the Babe did not disappoint his new team or his fans. In 1920 he hit 54 four-baggers, more than the total home run output of any other *team* in the American League. His batting average was .358, and his slugging average was an amazing .847, a record that has never been equaled. In 1921 he hit 59 homers and batted .378. The Yankees won their first pennant but lost the Series to their fellow New Yorkers, the Giants. The Yanks also made plans to build their own stadium just across the river from the Polo Grounds. In 1922 Ruth received a $52,000 salary, then the highest in history.

Even though his batting fell off, all of baseball was talking about Ruth and the home run. And that year the improved Yankees won their second straight pennant.

When the 1923 season opened, the new Yankee Stadium was ready. Universities all over America had been building big new stadiums for football, but the New York team was the first to do the same for baseball. The sparkling new park could hold nearly 70,000 fans, and few of them doubted that the reason for such an optimistic venture was Babe Ruth. In fact, Yankee Stadium became known as "The House That Ruth Built."

Wednesday, April 18, 1923, was raw and windy, but the stadium was filled with Yankee fans who had come to celebrate a great day and to see their hero in action. Could the spindle-legged Ruth rise to the occasion and christen the stadium with a home run in the first game?

He failed his first time up. But then in the third inning he came to the plate against his old Boston teammates with two Yanks on base. The pitcher was veteran Howard

Cars line up on the gravel roads outside the Stadium on opening day.

Ehmke. He worked the count on Ruth to two balls and two strikes. Then, according to a newspaper story, "Ehmke tried to fool him with a slow ball. The ball came in slowly, but it went out quite rapidly, rising on a line to land eight or ten rows behind the low railing in the bleachers. As Ruth circled the bases, he received probably the greatest ovation of his career."

The Yankees won the game 4–1, the proper start for a spectacular year. They finished the season 16 games ahead of the second place team. Ruth batted .398 and hit 41 homers. In six World Series games against the New York Giants, Ruth had two singles, a double, a triple and three home runs, as the Yanks won their first World Championship.

By the end of the season Ruth was considered the greatest sports hero of the age. Before he retired there would be more heroics and more controversy. But one hero was not enough for sports fans of the '20s, and others were arriving every year.

10

Four Horsemen and a Galloping Ghost

When Eastern sports fans opened their Sunday papers one morning in October 1924, the headline proclaimed that Army, one of the football powers of the day, had been upset by Notre Dame. Under the headline was this dispatch:

> Polo Grounds, New York, Oct. 18—Outlined against a blue-gray October sky, the Four Horsemen rode again. In dramatic lore they were known as Famine, Pestilence, Destruction and Death. These are only aliases. Their real names are Stuhldreher, Miller, Crowley and Layden. . . .

The author of these lines was Grantland Rice, one of the most widely read sportswriters of the era. Before the days of radio and television coverage, he and his colleagues told sports fans all they knew about their teams and heroes. And when a reporter of Rice's reputation began a story like this, it was inevitable that the four men involved would be known forever after as The Four Horsemen of Notre Dame.

The game itself had not even been that exciting. The precision play of Notre Dame

Sportswriter Grantland Rice seated at his typewriter in the press box.

Illinois' Red Grange (at left) carries for a touchdown against Michigan in 1924.

had defeated a heavier Army team 13–7. But when the Irish arrived back in South Bend, Indiana, an alert photographer who had seen Rice's story, posed Stuhldreher, Miller, Crowley and Layden on horses. The photograph was sent by wire to newspapers all over the country. The Notre Dame football team became a national favorite, partly because of its great football performances, and partly because Grantland Rice had begun his account of the Army game with a lively figure of speech.

That same week Grantland Rice would help create another legend. On the same afternoon as the Army-Notre Dame contest, another game halfway across the country created an even more famous football hero. Although Rice wasn't there to see it, he would suggest the nickname that would cling to this other hero as well.

In Champaign, Illinois, the University of Illinois was christening a new stadium in a game against Michigan. Some 64,000 fans were there at 2 P.M. when the referee blew his whistle and the Michigan kicker swung

his foot into the ball. It carried to the 5-yard-line where it landed in the arms of Number 77.

The Illinois fans already knew who 77 was, and before the day was over, so would the rest of the country's football fans. After he caught the ball he seemed to hesitate for a split-second. He took three strides to the right and then, strangely, cut back toward the center of the field. Fielding Yost, who was still the coach at Michigan, had promised that every time 77 had the ball "there will be eleven hard, clean Michigan tacklers headed for him at the same time." Now it seemed that all eleven were waiting for him.

The Illinois back burst away from the first two, spun to the left, then back to the right, leaving three Wolverines grasping for his shadow. An instant later he was in the clear, racing 95 yards for a touchdown.

Red Grange, who would make the number 77 the most famous in sports, had scored on his first play, leaving the eleven Michigan tacklers behind. But there was more to come.

The Illini kicked off to Michigan and

stopped the Wolverines cold. Michigan punted, and the ball was downed on the Illinois 33. On the first play from scrimmage, Grange took the ball and started around right end. Then after four steps he cut back over a hole in the Michigan line. The linemen lunged at him and missed. Then he stiff-armed a back. Two more defensive backs had a shot at him, but Grange eluded them to complete a 67-yard sprint for another touchdown.

Less than three minutes later Illinois had the ball again. Grange took the snap and slanted at tackle. This time he changed direction to the outside, got past the end and sped down the sidelines 56 yards for the score.

The Michigan offense sputtered once more, and Illinois took possession on the Wolverine 44-yard-line. The Michigan players were all up close to the line, determined to stop Grange. Red took the snap and went through the middle, preceded by

Off the field, Red smiles for a photographer.

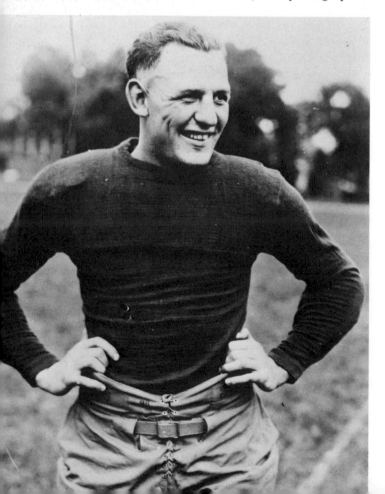

Illinois' great blocking fullback, Earl Britton. If it hadn't been for their loud cheers, the fans might have heard a *whooosh* as Grange sped between the Michigan defenders, faked his way past a back and raced 44 yards for his fourth touchdown.

Grange had touched the ball four times. And he had scored four touchdowns of 95, 67, 56 and 44 yards in just twelve minutes of play against a Michigan team that had been undefeated for almost three full seasons. It was the greatest display of ball-carrying in all of football's history.

After his last score, Grange leaned against the goal post gasping for breath. Bob Zuppke, the Illinois coach, took him out of the line-up for a rest. One sportswriter reported that the ovation Grange got as he trotted off the field was "something not heard since Caesar's return to Rome in triumph from the wars."

The amazing back returned to the game in the second half. He scored on a 15-yard run on his first play and later threw a touchdown pass for another. He carried the ball 21 times for 402 yards, and he had six pass completions for 64 yards, as Illinois destroyed Michigan, "hard, clean tacklers" and all, 39–14. Yet his second-half heroics were anti-climactic after the incredible four touchdowns in the first twelve minutes.

Later in 1924 Grange scored three long touchdowns against a great Chicago team to give Illinois a 21–21 tie. Then in 1925, as a senior, he made believers of the Eastern football fans in a game against Pennsylvania. The game was played in a pouring rain, and Grange's fans were afraid the muddy field would ruin his footing. But Red was a superman, and even the mud couldn't stop him. He carried for 363 yards and scored three touchdowns. In the pressbox after the game, Laurence Stallings, a famous playwright who was covering the game for a New York paper, stared helplessly at his typewriter. Finally, he pushed it aside. "I can't write it," he sighed. "This story is too big for me."

When the 1925 season ended, Grange left the University of Illinois and signed a professional contract with the Chicago Bears. Suddenly a team which had been playing to crowds of 5,000 or less was playing to 50,000 and more. Grange put pro football on the road to success.

But his greatest moment was still that amazing afternoon in 1924 when he had outrun and outscored the whole Michigan team. Shortly after that game the following verse had appeared in Grantland Rice's column:

A streak of fire, a breath of flame,
  Eluding all who reach and clutch;
A gray ghost thrown into the game,
  That rival hands may seldom touch.

Other writers picked up Rice's idea, and through the rest of his career Red Grange was known as "The Galloping Ghost."

11

The First King of Tennis

In 1925 Americans were finding new ways to use their growing leisure time. Automobiles had become so common that on Sunday afternoons the roads were filled with pleasure drivers. A growing number of people had radios, and this recent invention brought entertainment right into the house. With the turn of a dial, one could bring in music and news, and even "live" accounts of major sporting contests. Championship fights, the World Series, the Rose Bowl—suddenly these events had an audience of millions.

While the major spectator sports seemed to grow in popularity, other sports were gaining a following for the first time. In 1925 many Americans were talking about tennis. Until the 1920s tennis had always been a game for the rich. The man in the street connected the game with snobbery, didn't know deuce from a volley and didn't care. But with prosperity, thousands discovered they could afford to play tennis. Country clubs added new courts, and public ones were built all over the country. And as tennis became a major participant sport, attention turned to America's top player—Big Bill Tilden.

Tilden had burst upon the world of tennis

Big Bill Tilden during a 1923 match.

early in the decade. He was a tall, thin right-hander, whose giant strides covered ground with swiftness and grace. He had been born to a wealthy family and didn't have to worry about making a living—which was fortunate, since tennis was then a sport for amateurs only.

In 1920 Tilden won the men's singles at Wimbledon, England, the capital of world tennis, and he repeated that achievement in 1921. But he was even more impressive in the U.S. men's singles (played at Forest Hills, New York). After losing the 1919 finals to a veteran named Bill Johnston, Tilden went on to win five singles championships in the next five years.

Big Bill Tilden had tremendous tennis talent. His cannonball service was awesome, and he hit the ball with amazing power both forehand and backhand. Also a master of the chop and the slice, he was the most complete player the tennis world had ever seen.

But more important, Tilden was the most dramatic player ever to set foot on the court. Some said he was a frustrated actor—he had once had a small part in a Broadway play and he had lost a small fortune supporting plays that failed. But on the court his dramatic flair was far more successful.

Despite his great talents, Tilden often fell far behind in a match. Then he would come storming back at the last minute to win just when a victory seemed impossible. In one match he was behind two sets to none and had lost the first two games of the third set. All his opponent had to do was win four more games in the set to win the whole match. Tilden went to the sidelines, took a pitcher of ice water and poured it over his head. The respectful tennis audience tittered and whispered as he slowly dried himself off. Was he really in trouble? Or was he just acting?

Tilden went back to the court and won three straight sets!

Now in 1925 Tilden faced his old rival, Little Bill Johnston, in the men's singles at Forest Hills. Little Bill was half a foot shorter than Tilden, and despite his doggedly intense game, he had lost the American championship to Big Bill five straight years. Now he was getting old—it seemed likely that this would be his last year as a top competitor—and he wanted desperately to win back the singles title.

The 13,000 fans at Forest Hills knew that Tilden was the favorite. Still, he had barely scraped through his Davis Cup matches a week earlier, falling behind Frenchman Jean Borotra two sets to one before winning. And he had lost two straight sets to Rene Lacoste. In true Tilden form, he had then won three straight sets to win the match. But could a man be lucky enough or strong enough to come back like that in every match?

Tilden uses his height to return a high lob.

Little Bill Johnston came out fighting. He clearly dominated Tilden in the first set, which he won 6–4. The second set was tougher and went to deuce. Leading by nine games to eight, Johnston took the lead in the next game and had Tilden at set point. If he could take the next volley, Johnston would win the second set, and Tilden would be at a tremendous disadvantage.

But there are athletes who resist fate, and Big Bill Tilden was one of them. He kept Johnston from winning that set point and moments later won the game to tie the set at 9–9. Then he won the next two games—and the set—tying the match at one set apiece.

Johnston seemed to fold in the third set, losing 6–3. But just when his fans were about to count him out, he picked up and won the fourth set to tie Tilden once again. Now everything would be decided by the fifth set.

But Tilden was just too much, especially in a deciding set. He ran the tiring Johnston all over the court and finally won his sixth game and the match on a blinding service ace, his tenth of the afternoon. Tilden had won his sixth straight national singles crown, a record that has never been approached.

But if Tilden was the King of tennis, he had to share his rule with another American star—a young woman named Helen Wills.

12

Women in the Spotlight

Until 1920 all the lawmakers of the United States were men, and they were all elected by men. Only a few years earlier the idea that a woman could hold office or even vote would have been laughed at. But the role of women was changing rapidly. In 1920 they voted in their first presidential election, and in 1925 Wyoming (which had given women the right to vote in state elections in 1875) elected Nellie Tayloe Ross governor.

The changes went beyond the political realm. During the 1920s the number of working women increased rapidly. More and more women enrolled at colleges and universities. Many institutions became "co-educational," adopting the revolutionary plan of educating women right alongside men.

As women began to make their marks in other pursuits, they began to surface in sports. One of the few games with wide female participation was tennis, so it was fitting that Helen Wills, the first nationally known woman athlete, was a tennis player —perhaps the greatest in American history.

She came to Forest Hills in 1923, when she was 17, wearing pig-tails and the green eyeshade that would become her trademark. She won the women's singles championship, causing a mild sensation. Soon sportswriters were referring to the intense new champion as "Little Miss Poker Face." And before long, Helen Wills was a national celebrity.

She returned to Forest Hills in 1924 and 1925 to win the singles championships again. She and Bill Tilden were acknowledged as the top American stars of the game.

But Miss Wills had serious competition from overseas. Many claimed that the greatest woman player in the world was Suzanne Lenglen of France. Others favored Helen Wills. To settle the matter, a special match was arranged between the two champions early in 1926 at the French resort of Cannes. News of the match traveled around the world. Long before the appointed date it was impossible to get hotel rooms within 50 miles of the city. The world's most expensive yachts were anchored in the Mediterranean near Cannes,

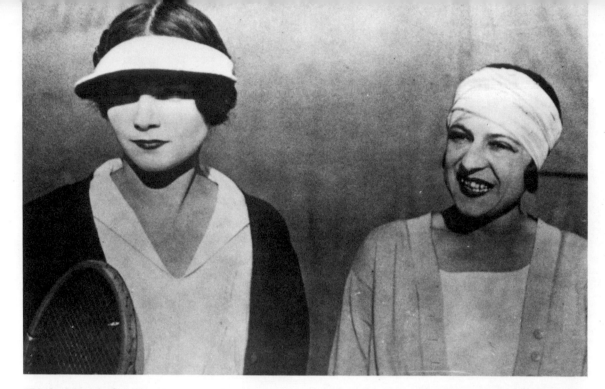

"Little Miss Poker Face" poses with champion Suzanne Lenglen before their 1926 competition.

and their owners talked endlessly about Lenglen and Wills, betting huge sums of money on the outcome of the game. Not until the Bobby Riggs–Billie Jean King match nearly 50 years later would a woman tennis player participate in such a highly publicized match.

Yet Helen Wills was only 19 years old. Under the glaring scrutiny of the world press and in the whirl of pre-match parties, Helen lost her nerve. In the circus-like atmosphere, Miss Lenglen swept to victory.

When she returned home, Helen was still a heroine, but her reputation had been slightly tarnished. Soon after, she wound up in the hospital, suffering from appendicitis and then from complications after surgery. The 1926 tennis season came and went, and Helen Wills never appeared. Would she be back the next season? After her illness, would she ever again show the blazing power that had revolutionized women's tennis? While her fans were wondering about her future, world attention shifted to another young woman performing on a very different athletic stage.

The appetite of sports fans in the '20s was so great that promoters and individuals scheduled many kinds of sports spectaculars.

One event that caught the public imagination was the endurance contest. In the spirit of the *Guinness Book of Records,* some people competed to see who could sit for the longest time on top of a flagpole, while others went in for marathon dancing. But the most durable of the endurance competitions was long-distance swimming.

In 1875 an Englishman named Captain Matthew Webb had become the first person ever to swim across the English Channel, a 21-mile stretch of icy water between Cape Gris-Nez in France and the Dover shore in England. In the succeeding years few had been crazy enough to try the amazing feat. But when the 1920s arrived, interest in swimming the Channel revived. By 1926 five men had crossed successfully, and the time record was set in 1923 by Sebastian Tirabocchi of Italy, who made the journey in 16 hours, 23 minutes.

No one knows for sure how many swimmers started the Channel swim and failed. For centuries the Channel crossing had been notorious for its dangerous currents, its ugly storms and its cold waters. If it was treacherous to boatmen, what could a lone swimmer expect?

At 7 A.M. on August 6, 1926, a most unlikely swimmer stood on a French beach

Gertrude Ederle is coated with grease just before entering the English Channel in 1926.

18 hours or more after she left Cape Gris-Nez.

At 7:09 Trudy jumped into the water and began the swim. Painted on the side of the *Alsace* was a sign, "This Way, Ol' Girl!", and an arrow pointing straight ahead. She followed the sign with a strong crawl stroke.

After the first hour her trainer shouted instructions from the tug for Trudy to slow down. If she started out too fast, she would never have the energy to finish. But Trudy refused. To help pass the monotonous hours in the icy water, her father, a sister and two swimmers in training for the Channel crossing sang songs to her from the tug and shouted encouragement.

At 10 o'clock Miss Ederle had her first meal, sipping some beef extract through a straw. The radioman on the *Alsace* included this bit of news in his hourly report. At 1:30 she had already covered 12 of the 21 miles. At that rate she would arrive in England after less than 12 hours of swimming. But those who knew Channel swimming realized that the worst was yet to come.

Soon it began to rain. Fierce winds raised swells which threatened to engulf the lone swimmer. Now the currents, which had been helping her along, would turn against her. Unless she could hold her own against those

near Cape Gris-Nez, ready to make the swim. She was a stocky 5-foot-5 New Yorker dressed in a red bathing suit and smeared with grease from head to toe to protect her from the cold water ahead. Her name was Gertrude Ederle, and she was 19 years old.

A woman swimming the English Channel? The idea would have been even more startling if Trudy Ederle had not already tried the same feat (and failed) the year before. This time millions of fans around the world were waiting to hear if she could do it. In fact, interest was so great that arrangements had been made to send hourly reports of her progress by radio from the tugboat *Alsace,* which would accompany her on the crossing. It was thought that if she made it at all, Trudy Ederle would arrive on the shores of England after midnight,

Trudy swims alongside the tugboat Alsace *as her supporters cheer her on.*

52   currents, they would carry her miles off-course. (It was estimated that Captain Webb, the original Channel swimmer, had actually swum 39 miles to cross the 21-mile wide stretch of water.)

Between 1:30 and 5 o'clock Trudy battled the waves and currents and gained about three miles. But she still had six miles to go. The winds increased, and the cold sea was getting wilder by the minute. At times, her supporters on the tugboat lost sight of her. Someone suggested she give up. "No! No!" she shouted over and over.

By 6:30 Trudy had left the most treacherous currents behind, and she struck out for the English shore. Meanwhile, thousands of people began to gather on the beach, hoping to see her arrive. They had come early, not wanting to miss any of the drama.

Then word came that she had passed just south of Goodwin Lightship, only a mile or two from shore. A tremendous cheer went up, and hundreds of drivers blew automobile horns. Some even sent up flares, hoping to encourage her. Trudy Ederle needed only to fight the numbing cold and the waves for two more miles.

At about 9:30 the *Alsace* loomed out of the darkness, less than half a mile from shore. It anchored there, and a few minutes later, those nearest the surf caught sight of Trudy herself. Hundreds of flashlights picked her out of the gloom as she stroked slowly toward shallow water. People waded into the seas fully clothed to help her as her feet touched ground, but she stumbled ashore without aid and was quickly wrapped in blankets.

From the time she slipped into the water in France until she touched the sand on the Dover shore, 14 hours and 31 minutes had passed. Not only had Trudy Ederle swum the Channel, she had beaten the former record-holder—a man—by nearly two hours.

After a brief rest, Gertrude Ederle was taken by boat to the port of Dover. British

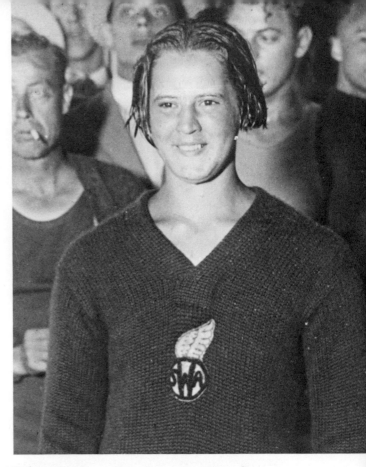

Young Trudy smiles after winning a distance swim in her native New York.

customs officials wanted to see her passport. One of them even asked Trudy where she had come from and what means of transportation she had used. After Trudy's admiring British fans convinced the officials that she really *had* swum the Channel, she was admitted to England and given a proper welcome.

That winter Helen Wills began training for the 1927 tennis season. After a long convalescence, she came back into form slowly. Although she had a successful spring and summer season, some observers felt she was lacking the intensity she had shown in 1925. Did she have the necessary stamina to compete in a long tournament? Did she still have the killer instinct that had once led a sportswriter to describe her as "lovely, calm, cold, efficient, ruthless, aloof"?

The answers to these questions would come on the courts at Forest Hills in August of 1927 in the women's national singles championship. Helen Wills marched through the preliminary rounds as if she had never been away. She faced five opponents and beat each of them in two straight sets. No set ever went to deuce, and Little Miss Poker Face lost only 13 games while winning 60.

But there was another competitor—a surprising 16-year-old named Betty Nuthall of Great Britain—who looked as good as Miss Wills. On her way to the finals Miss Nuthall had crushed every opponent. And a few weeks earlier she had upset Molla Bjurstedt Mallory, the winner of the 1926 U.S. championship. In many ways the young Englishwoman resembled the Helen Wills of 1923, who had won her first Forest Hills championship at 17.

Now Helen's fans and critics would find out if she had lost her magic. When the time arrived for the women's finals, Miss Wills adjusted her green eyeshade and took the court against Miss Nuthall.

The first set lasted just twelve minutes! Helen Wills blasted the ball—"just like a man," some said—time and again, running her younger opponent all over the court and winning the set 6–1.

"Such a pounding as the ball received in that final seldom if ever has been duplicated in any women's match," wrote one reporter. "Miss Nuthall, with an everything-to-gain-and-nothing-to-lose attitude, waded into Miss Wills' fiercest drives—and was smothered."

In the second set Miss Nuthall tried to keep Helen off-balance with soft returns. The strategy worked briefly, but soon Wills

Looking more like a dancer than a tennis player, Helen Wills wins the nationals.

was slamming the ball again, rushing the net, forcing the game and keeping Miss Nuthall on the defensive. Helen won the set 6–4, and with it the match and the singles championship.

And Little Miss Poker Face would accomplish much more. In 1927 she went to Wimbledon, England, and won her first British singles championship, symbolic of world supremacy. She retired in 1938, having won the Wimbledon title eight times. By that time she was called Little Miss Poker Face less often. A new title had been invented. Helen Wills had become "Queen Helen," the most illustrious woman in tennis history.

13

Champs and Challengers

The year 1927 was special, even for the remarkable decade of the 1920s. In May a young man named Charles Lindbergh electrified America and Europe by flying—all alone in a single-engined plane—from New York to Paris. After receiving a tu-

multuous welcome in France, he returned to one of the greatest public celebrations ever held in New York.

Lindbergh set a heroic tone for the year, and sports fans had many of their own heroes to choose from. Helen Wills won her first Wimbledon championship. Bobby Jones was outclassing all opposition in the increasingly popular game of golf. A new hockey player named Eddie Shore was revolutionizing hockey. And Red Grange was a big attraction in the young National Football League.

But in sports, the year belonged to two giants and two young challengers. The giants were Jack Dempsey and Babe Ruth. The challengers were Gene Tunney and Lou Gehrig.

Late in September, all eyes turned toward Soldiers Field in Chicago. There, on the evening of September 22, one of the greatest heavyweight fights of the era had been planned by master promoter Tex Rickard: a rematch between champion Gene Tunney and ex-champ Jack Dempsey.

Dempsey had been the dominant fighter of the decade. After winning the heavyweight championship from Jess Willard in 1919, he made several famous defenses. In 1921 he knocked out the handsome French champion, Georges Carpentier, in four rounds. For the first time in boxing history, the fans paid over a million dollars to see a fight.

Two years later, on September 14, 1923, Dempsey met "The Wild Bull of the Pampas," Argentinian Luis Firpo. The fight lasted only four minutes, but it was one of the most spectacular in history. In the first round, Firpo knocked Dempsey clear out of the ring.

Sportswriters in the first row lifted the champ back into the ring before the count of ten. But in the same round Dempsey, in his meanest mood, knocked Firpo down a total of six times. Instead of going to a neutral corner when Firpo was down, Jack stood over him and hit him again the minute the South American climbed to his feet. Dempsey had broken the rules, but no one noticed. Firpo came out for the second round—but was hammered to the canvas again. He got up, but the second time he went down, he was out cold.

After the Firpo fight Dempsey retired from the ring. He married a glamorous movie star and didn't fight again until 1926. This time he was to meet a new challenger —young, attractive Gene Tunney. As usual, Dempsey was cast as the villain and his opponent was the Knight in Shining Armor. Tunney had been a Marine during the World War (Dempsey had avoided the service) and had been world light heavyweight champ. He was a clever boxer, but few thought he would stand a chance against the murderous Dempsey.

The fight was a scheduled ten-rounder in Philadelphia's Municipal Stadium. Tex Rickard boasted it would be the first fight with a *two*-million dollar gate. Fans were hoping for a miracle, but expecting Dempsey to win easily.

From the first bell, Tunney outclassed Dempsey, making the champ look awkward and crude. As the fight wore on, it became clear that Dempsey was not in top condition. Tunney connected again and again with stiff left jabs and right hooks. In the fourth round it began to rain. Dempsey slipped and slid around the ring, but the wet surface didn't bother the younger fighter.

Dempsey's face was a bloody pulp by the tenth round. Had the fight been scheduled for 15 rounds, he surely would have been knocked out. After the decision was announced, Dempsey's trainers had to lead him from the arena. The defeated champ's face was so swollen he could hardly see.

Now it was a year later—September 22, 1927. Tunney, the new champion, and Dempsey, the former champ, were meeting again. No one had ever won back the heavyweight title after losing it, but many fans believed that Dempsey could do it. He had been in rigorous training and was in much better condition than the year before. And his loss seemed to have softened public attitudes toward him. Now that he was the challenger, more people seemed to be rooting for him.

At left, Jack Dempsey stands over Tunney after knocking him down. At right, the referee delays his count, insisting that Dempsey go to a neutral corner first.

Soldiers' Field in Chicago held 105,000 people that night, the largest crowd ever to witness a boxing match. The interest in the first fight had been intense, but this time the whole country was waiting to hear the result.

Dempsey was sharper this time, but he was still no match for the younger, cleverer Tunney. As in their first match, Tunney danced out of harm's way and landed a good number of his own punches. After six rounds it was clear that Tunney would win —unless Dempsey could connect with one of his crushing blows.

Then suddenly, in the seventh round, Dempsey landed a hard left hook flush to Tunney's jaw. (Tunney later revealed that there had been a fuzzy spot in his vision from a practice injury and that he had never seen the punch coming.) Now Tunney was in a daze and Dempsey moved in for the kill, throwing punch after punch to follow up his advantage. He must have known that this was his first and perhaps only chance to win. Finally, Tunney tumbled to the canvas in a sitting position, clutching the ropes. The referee moved in to begin the count.

But Dempsey, as in previous fights, was so eager for the kill that he stood over Tunney waiting for him to get up. This time the referee, who had been warned about

Jack's reluctance to retreat to a neutral corner, refused to start the count. He motioned to Dempsey to move back, but at first he got no response. It took four or five seconds for Dempsey to realize what was happening.

Finally, after what seemed an age, Dempsey retreated and the count began. When the referee counted "nine," Tunney pulled himself to his feet. The roar of the huge crowd was deafening. Tunney was clear-headed enough to defend himself and stay out of danger, while Dempsey chased him, trying to land a knockout blow. At one point, Dempsey stopped and motioned to Tunney to come and fight—but it was the gesture of a frustrated man. Finally the bell sounded and the round was over.

Tunney came out for the eighth round with renewed confidence, and for the rest of the fight he punished Dempsey. When it was over, there was no doubt about the verdict—Gene Tunney had given the ex-champ another terrible beating and had retained his heavyweight crown.

But almost immediately, fans began to argue about the knockdown in the seventh round. Films showed that Tunney was down on the canvas for 14 seconds. If Dempsey had moved to the neutral corner at once, could Tunney have gotten up? Many who

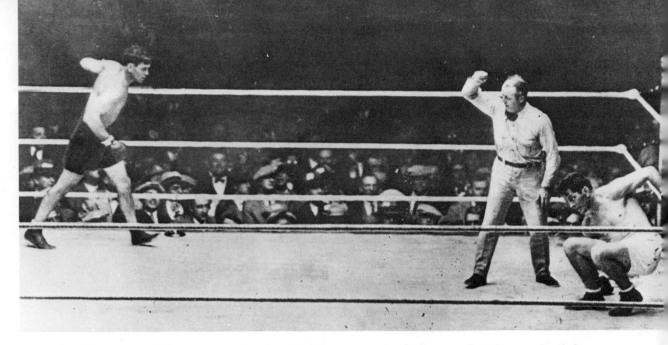

After the "long count," Dempsey rushes in, but Tunney survived the round and won the fight.

were there doubted it. They claimed that Dempsey's intense desire to win had lost him the fight. Tunney claimed he could have gotten up any time he wanted. The incident provided one of the great controversies of sport. But few spectators could deny that Tunney had won the match fairly and deserved the heavyweight crown. Jack Dempsey, one of the great champions of the age, was finished.

In baseball, the story all year had been the Yankees. Boasting one of the greatest line-ups in the history of the game, they had run away from the rest of the league. Their biggest star was young first baseman Lou Gehrig. As the season neared its end, he was leading the league in batting average and had driven in more than 150 runs. Since early in 1925 he had been a Yankee regular, and his performance had been so consistent and spectacular that some suggested he would soon take over for Babe Ruth himself.

The Babe was still the giant of the diamond. But his seasons seemed to alternate —one good, then one bad. He was 32, and as he grew older, his pot belly grew larger and he looked less and less like an athlete. The 1927 season was turning out to be a good one, although he was not approaching any of the records he had set in the past. On

September 1, he had 43 homers and was well on his way to another season total of 50 or more.

Then in a few short weeks, the Babe outdid himself and made the world forget Lou Gehrig. He went on an amazing home run spree, hitting 13 in the first three weeks of September. On the day of the Dempsey-Tunney fight, he hit his 56th of the season.

Suddenly it seemed that he could break one of his old records. With five games left to play, he needed four homers to break his single season mark of 59. For other hitters such a feat would be impossible. But it seemed that nothing was really impossible for the Babe.

In the next two games he failed. Doubters counted Ruth out—now he needed four homers in three games. On September 27, however, hitting against the great Lefty Grove, Ruth kept his slim hopes alive by slamming one into the seats. The next day against the Washington Senators he hit two more to tie his old record at 59.

That left one game. The Yankees were facing the Senators in Yankee Stadium. Every time Ruth came to the plate, he was cheered by thousands of fans who were there to see if he could hit his 60th. But no home runs came. In three times up Ruth had a walk and two singles.

In the eighth inning he came to bat with

the score tied 2–2. Unless the game went into extra innings, this would be his last time up for the season. The roar of the crowd was deafening. Washington pitcher Tom Zachary threw a screwball that broke over the plate. The umpire called "Strike one!" and the crowd groaned.

The second pitch was another screwball, but this time the Babe was swinging. He pulled the ball straight down the right-field line. It was far enough, but would it be fair or foul? All eyes were on umpire Bill Dineen as the ball landed in the stands. Then he signaled—fair ball!—and the crowd roared.

The first man to shake Ruth's hand as he crossed the plate was the other Yankee star, Lou Gehrig. Lou had hit .378 for the season, driven in a record-breaking 175 runs and hit 47 homers—one of the greatest seasons on record. He was voted Most Valuable Player for his accomplishments.

But still, Babe Ruth got the attention. The 1927 season was remembered not for Gehrig's great performances. It was remembered because that was the year the Babe, colorful and dramatic as ever, hit 60 home runs.

Babe Ruth, the "Sultan of Swat," watches his 60th home run rocket toward the stands.

14

The Gray-Haired Goalie

The big new car of 1928 was the Model A Ford. The Ford Model T had been manufactured virtually unchanged for 15 years, so when the company announced a new model, to be unveiled on December 2, 1927, people stormed Ford showrooms. In New York, Detroit, Chicago and other major cities, police had to be called out to manage the huge crowds—some estimated at more than 100,000.

The big new sport of 1928 was hockey. Hockey first emerged in Canada. But in the mid-1920s the professional National Hockey League expanded, adding teams in New York, Boston, Pittsburgh, Detroit and Chicago. Since basketball was still in its infancy and was not considered a serious sport, hockey was bidding to become the major winter sport, bridging the gap between the end of the football season and the beginning of baseball.

The most successful American teams were the Boston Bruins, the NHL's American Division leaders in 1927–28, and the

New York Rangers. The Rangers, coached by Lester Patrick, finished second to the Bruins in the regular season. But in the post-season playoffs for the Stanley Cup, the symbol of hockey supremacy, Patrick's Rangers defeated Pittsburgh and Boston. Those victories put the New Yorkers into the final round against the Montreal Maroons and gave them a chance to be the first American winners of the Stanley Cup.

The Rangers played their regular home games in Madison Square Garden in New York. But when they made the playoff finals, the Garden was already occupied by a circus. So all games of the best-of-five series would be played in Montreal. Despite this disadvantage, Ranger fans were confident that their team could bring the Cup to the United States.

The Maroons won the first game 2–0. Then in the second game, the Rangers were faced with another terrible disadvantage. Four minutes into the second period the Maroons' great forward Nels Stewart fired a shot at the Ranger goal. New York goalie Lorne Chabot stopped the puck—with his head—and fell unconscious to the ice.

The puck had opened an ugly cut just over Chabot's eye, and he was rushed to the hospital. Now Ranger manager Lester Patrick had a problem. Like most other teams, the Rangers carried only one goalie on the squad. The rules for the Cup playoffs said that Patrick could substitute another goalie—if he could find one and if the opposing manager gave his permission.

In the stands that night, as a spectator, was Alex Connell, a goalie from the NHL's Ottawa team. Patrick asked Maroon manager Eddie Gerard for permission to use him. Gerard, an old enemy of Patrick's, smiled and refused. There was another minor-league goalie in the crowd. Again Patrick asked, and again Gerard refused.

Patrick boiled with rage as he took his team to the dressing room. Montreal fans, sensing that the Rangers might never recover from the loss of Chabot, started a chorus of hoots and cheers.

While the team and Patrick were trying to decide what to do, a New York sportswriter named Jim Burchard poked his head into the Ranger huddle. "Hey, Les, why don't you put the pads on yourself?" he

Goalie Lorne Chabot, whose injury paved the way for the gray-haired goalie.

asked Patrick with a smile. "You can do it!"

No one ever determined whether or not Burchard was kidding. But Patrick took the suggestion seriously. Finally the silver-haired manager said, "He's right. I'm putting on the pads."

Of course, Patrick knew that the hockey goalie has one of the most demanding jobs in sport. He must be strong enough to wear the heaviest pads on ice for a full game of bone-crunching action. He must be agile as a cat and have lightning reflexes. Above all, he must be fearless in the face of charging players and a puck that can travel at 100 miles per hour.

Yet here was a 44-year-old man—he was called "The Silver Fox" partly because of his distinguished gray hair—skating awkwardly onto the ice in pads that were way too big for him. Lester Patrick had played no hockey for years and had played in goal only once or twice in his life. But now he was going to play in a Stanley Cup finals match!

Fans roared at the incredible sight. The other Rangers nervously slapped a few easy practice shots at Patrick to get him warmed up. There were still almost two full periods of hockey to play. Would poor Lester even be standing up by the end?

When the game resumed, the Montreal forwards, led by the magnificent Nels Stewart, stormed the Ranger goal, hoping to bury the old man under a barrage of shots. The Rangers, understandably, played a conservative defensive game, hoping to help their old goalie out as much as possible. But Patrick hung on, and at the end of the period the game was still scoreless.

Early in the third period the Rangers scored. After ten minutes their lead still held. Patrick was heroically deflecting shot after shot. But could he hold up for the rest of the game?

Then with 5:40 left to play, the Maroons' Stewart slammed the puck past Patrick and into the net to tie the score. Regulation time

Manager Lester Patrick in goal for the Rangers.

ended, and the teams had one goal apiece.

Then, as now, playoff games that ended tied went into sudden-death overtime—the first goal scored would win the game. Stewart and his fellow attackers tried again and again to crack the Ranger defense, but without success. Finally, after 7:05 in overtime, the star of the New Yorkers, Frank Boucher, scored and won the amazing game for the Rangers. Lester Patrick had held. As his team carried him off on their shoulders, the aging coach had tears in his eyes—tears of joy and exhaustion and perhaps relief.

Somewhat sheepishly, Montreal gave permission for the Rangers to use a minor league goalie, Joe Miller, in the third game. The Rangers lost. By that time, however, Lorne Chabot had recovered enough to return. The Rangers, with their own goalie back in the nets, won the fourth and fifth games to take the Stanley Cup.

Thanks to the courage of the silver-haired Patrick, the Rangers became the first American team to carry the Stanley Cup out of Canada.

15

"Turn Around!"

Perhaps it was only proper that sports in the 1920s should close out the decade on the kind of zany note that was typical of the whole Golden Decade. Nobody planned it that way. Nobody could have counted on it.

The 101,000 people who streamed into the Rose Bowl in Pasadena, California, on New Year's Day, 1929, certainly anticipated a great football game. The University of California had an All-America end in Irvin Phillips, a fine halfback in Benny Lom and an outstanding center in Roy Riegels. Their opponents, Georgia Tech, had three All-Americas including halfback Warner Mizell, who had led the Engineers to an unbeaten season.

Georgia Tech was a slight favorite, yet many experts thought Cal's Golden Bears were strong enough to upset the Engineers. There was still only one bowl game on New Year's Day. All the others—the Orange Bowl, Sugar Bowl, Cotton Bowl and the rest—had not yet been started, so the attention of the entire nation was focused on the game in Pasadena.

In addition to the live crowd, millions of people were listening to the radio account —and they were about to hear something they would find hard to believe.

In the second quarter, with the game scoreless, Georgia Tech had the ball on its own 40. A Tech ball-carrier drove into the Golden Bear line. As he was tackled, he fumbled the ball. Football players played both offense and defense in those days, so it was Roy Riegels, the California center, who lunged for the ball.

Riegels scooped it up on a good bounce and headed for the Georgia Tech goal. (College rules then allowed a player to run with a recovered fumble.) Riegels was hit immediately by a Tech lineman but spun around and got free. Then he took off for the goal line 60 yards away.

But something was wrong. Not a single Georgia Tech tackler was pursuing Riegels. The only player who was chasing him was his own teammate, halfback Benny Lom. Lom was screaming, "Turn around! Turn around!"

Roy Riegels carries along the sidelines (left), spins to avoid a tackler (right) . . .

But Riegels couldn't hear him over the roar of the crowd.

Roy Riegels was running the wrong way. He didn't realize that when he had spun away from the Tech tackler he had headed in the wrong direction—toward the California goal.

Riegels ran as fast as he could, trying to outrace the pounding feet behind him. Luckily, Benny Lom was a little faster than Riegels. Finally he caught up with him, but didn't dare dive for him—he might cause Riegels to fumble and allow Tech to recover the ball over the goal line for a touchdown. Lom grabbed Riegels' shoulder while yelling in his ear, then finally pulled him down on the California 2-yard-line.

The crowd could hardly believe what it had just seen. The radio announcer stuttered and did his best to explain to the fans listening at home. Riegels sat there on the ground, stunned by his mistake. His teammates gathered around to console him, but they were in a desperate spot. They would have to punt from their own end zone.

A few moments later Riegels made the long snap back to Benny Lom, who was to punt. Riegels was a fine center, but he was so shaken by his big mistake that his snap was off the mark. Lom couldn't get the ball off in time. The whole Tech line swarmed in and blocked the kick. The ball rolled out of the end zone for an automatic safety. Georgia Tech went ahead 2–0.

Tech scored a touchdown in the third quarter but missed the point after, so they led 8–0.

California scored in the fourth quarter on a pass from Lom to Irv Phillips, and converted. The game ended in an 8–7 victory for Tech. The margin of victory, of course, had been the safety.

Roy Riegels had gone on to play an outstanding game in the second half and would become an All-Coast center the following season. But as long as he lived, whenever his football career came up, he was remembered as the man who ran the wrong way in the Rose Bowl game.

Riegels wasn't the only thing that ran the wrong way in 1929. The stock market had been spiraling upward since 1923, making many people millionaires and encouraging millions of Americans to invest their money. But in September 1929 it turned around, and on October 29—which came to be known as Black Tuesday—the bottom fell out. Men who had been millionaires one day were paupers the next. Banks failed, millions were laid off their jobs and many committed suicide. The great business boom of the 1920s was over. Scarcely two months before the official end of the decade, the Roaring Twenties gave way to the Great Depression.

. . . dashes for the wrong goal (left) and is finally brought down by Benny Lom (right).

PART IV
1930-1939

The change from charming nonsense to misery and hardship happened in a hurry. By the end of 1929 three million wage-earners were out of work. By 1932 there were twelve million unemployed, and those who still had jobs worked shorter hours at reduced pay. Every segment of society suffered—from stockbrokers to farmers, from bankers to industrial workers. The government, led by President Hoover, seemed powerless to help. Clusters of tarpaper shacks for the homeless grew up on the edges of cities and even in city parks, and in the wry humor of the day they were called "Hoovervilles."

Hoover ran for reelection in 1932 but was soundly defeated by Franklin D. Roosevelt, who promised sweeping government actions to relieve the suffering of the unemployed and get the nation back on a sound economic footing. When he took office in March 1933, he told the American people, "The only thing we have to fear is fear itself." Within weeks he became the first president to make full use of radio, speaking to the nation in a series of "Fireside Chats" which sought to revive a sense of hope in America's future.

Still, even in the midst of misery, life went on. The prohibition of alcoholic beverages, which had gone into effect in 1920, had become a farce. When liquor was illegal, many people drank more of it than ever. And it was supplied by gangsters like Chicago's Al Capone, who made fabulous profits as a bootlegger. In 1933, during Roosevelt's first year as President, Prohibition was finally repealed.

In 1931 the 102-story Empire State Building, which had been planned before the Crash, became the tallest building in the world. John D. Rockefeller, Jr., was planning a whole complex of new office buildings and shops for New York. It was called Rockefeller Center. In 1934 nylon was invented, revolutionizing the women's stocking industry. Within 15 years silk stockings would be obsolete.

The film industry was becoming more sophisticated, and the decade became a golden age of film climaxed in 1939 by the release of "Gone with the Wind,"

a Civil War epic starring the nation's biggest box-office favorite, Clark Gable. The recording industry came into its own, and the new "big band" sound of Glenn Miller and the Dorsey brothers attracted the young to dance palaces and amusement parks. The top singer of the era was Bing Crosby. On the radio, comedy helped lighten the seriousness of the era. Amos & Andy, Jack Benny and Fred Allen were heard by millions.

Sport, too, survived, although it shared in the economic hardships of the nation. Professional football and college basketball became major attractions. Baseball stadiums installed lights and introduced night games. The popularity of Olympic competition increased tremendously when the 1932 Games were held in Los Angeles. And although there were no more "spectaculars" like the Dempsey-Tunney fights, boxing continued to attract a huge following.

Meanwhile, the events in world affairs were ominous. Germany, which had suffered terribly in the 1920s, was taken over by Adolf Hitler and his Nazi party. Dictator Benito Mussolini seized control of Italy. Both nations began to re-arm. Hitler based his rule on the theory of racial supremacy, claiming that men not of "Aryan" stock (Negroes, Jews and others) were inferior. Soon he was persecuting the large Jewish population of Germany, and many Jews fled to the United States and other countries.

As the decade drew to its close, Americans realized that another terrible war was brewing. As in 1914, they were reluctant at first to get into it. But when Adolf Hitler's armies invaded Poland in 1939, Great Britain and France declared war. Little less than a year later, Hitler had overrun France, Belgium, Holland and Denmark, and the British were holding out alone. Meanwhile, Japan had invaded China, threatening war in Asia as well. America began a crash program to arm itself and to provide weapons and armaments to its allies.

The 1930s, which had begun with the misery of a Great Depression, ended on a somber note. Few doubted that war—another great World War—was just ahead.

16

The Grand Slam of Golf

Before 1920 most Americans considered golf a foolish game. Who would want to chase a little white ball over hill and dale, hitting it with a stick, they asked? But during the prosperous '20s the game caught on in a big way. Country clubs sprang up all over the nation, and many cities and towns installed public courses. By the end of the decade hundreds of thousands were out on the golf course as often as they could manage, chasing the little white ball and hitting it with a stick.

Golf even became a big spectator sport. The major amateur tournaments were reported on the sports pages, and soon a series of professional tournaments was established as well. Manufacturers of golf equipment were willing to pay large sums to professionals who would endorse a club or a ball.

But the greatest golfer of the era was and always remained an amateur. He was first seen by the golfing public in the U. S. Amateur Golf Tournament at the Merion Cricket Club in Pennsylvania in 1916. He won two rounds of match play before being eliminated—not bad for a 14-year-old.

The golfer's name was Bobby Jones. Seven years later, when he was a student in law school, Jones won the U. S. Open, defeating the best amateurs and professionals in the land. By the end of 1929 he had won the U. S. Open twice more, the U. S. Ama-

Bobby Jones takes a shot at the 1930 British Amateur at Hoylake, England.

teur four times and the British Open twice. Jones was to golf what Ruth was to baseball, Tilden and Wills were to tennis and Grange was to football—the champ.

But Bobby Jones saved his greatest performance for the somber year of 1930. By then many businessmen-golfers were on the streets looking for jobs, not on the golf courses. But they could still afford to follow Jones, the greatest in the game, in his greatest triumph.

The drama began in May when Jones sunk an eight-foot putt on the last hole of the British Open at St. Andrews, Scotland, to tie British star Cyril Tolley. Jones beat Tolley in a playoff. A month later he battled gale-force winds at Hoylake, England, to win the British Open and become the first man ever to win the two big British tournaments in the same year.

Now sportswriters began speculating about Bobby's chances of completing a Grand Slam of golf by winning the U. S. Open and Amateur titles. No one had ever come close to winning the four biggest tournaments in one year. But here was Bobby Jones with two down and two to go.

The U. S. Open was played in July at the Interlachen course near Minneapolis. All the great names of golf were entered: Horton Smith, Harry Cooper, Tommy Armour and many more. Their pride was at stake because they were professionals and Jones still insisted on remaining an amateur, turning down tournament prizes and offers from golf equipment manufacturers.

A sizzling heat wave hit Minnesota the week of the big tournament. If the pros couldn't beat Bobby by themselves, maybe the weather would help. One day when the temperature went over 100, O. B. Keeler, the golf writer of the Atlanta *Constitution,* followed Bobby into the locker room after the round. He found Jones trying to undo his tie, which was soaked with perspiration. Keeler finally helped Jones cut the tie off with a knife.

"When are you going to quit this life?" Keeler asked.

Jones shook his head wearily. "Soon, I think . . ."

The answer made Keeler wonder if Jones would retire after the season. But first there was the Grand Slam to consider.

Jones had shot a 71 and a 73 on the first two rounds despite the heat. Still, he was two strokes behind Horton Smith and tied with Harry Cooper. But on the third round his competitors fell apart, and the amazing Jones shot a remarkable 68. Coming from two strokes behind, he had fashioned a five-stroke lead.

On the final day Jones almost fell apart himself as the golf world watched with anticipation. He was way over par after 13 holes, but he birdied the 14th and 16th holes. On the 18th he coolly sank a 40-foot putt for another birdie to finish the round with a creditable 75. He won the Open by two strokes, and his fans breathed a sigh of relief.

The year came to a climax in September, when Jones returned to the same Merion club where he had made his debut 14 years earlier. This time there were 18,000 fans—the largest gallery in golf history—waiting to see if the 28-year-old Jones could win the U. S. Amateur Tournament and complete the Grand Slam. Also present was a squad of United States Marines. But they weren't there to watch—they were there to protect Bobby Jones from his enthusiastic admirers.

In those days the Amateur was a match-play tournament. Rather than add up the number of strokes for a round, golfers played directly against each other to see who could win the most holes. As soon as a golfer had won enough holes to assure his victory, the match was over.

In the first round, Jones played against a Canadian, Ross Somerville. With four holes left, Jones was ahead by five, so the match was over and Jones had won, 5 and 4 (five holes ahead with four to play). That same afternoon he took on another opponent and again won 5 to 4.

After a third victory he swamped Jess Sweetser 9 and 8. This was golf's equivalent of the one-hitter. Jones had won nine of the first ten holes, so of course there was no reason to continue. Jones had eliminated four opponents and qualified to face Gene Homans in the final round of 36 holes.

Jones took an early advantage and gradually increased it. After the 28th hole, Jones was eight holes up with eight to play. Now he was assured of a tie. If he could win or tie one more hole, he would complete the Grand Slam. The gallery pressed close around the golfers as fans craned their necks to get the best views.

On the 29th Jones hit a long, straight drive. On his second shot he pitched onto the green, 20 feet from the cup. Homans also reached the green in two but was faced with a very long putt. He would have to drop it or lose the match. Jones tapped his approach to within a couple feet of the cup. Homans concentrated hard and finally stroked his ball toward the hole. It angled off to the side. He knew the match was over. Conceding the short putt to Jones, he strode over to congratulate him. The roar from the crowd was deafening, and fans began to converge on Jones.

But before they could get there, the Marines sprang into a circle around him—to protect the only man ever to score the Grand Slam of golf.

A few weeks later, Bobby Jones announced his retirement. He was 28 years old and had no worlds left to conquer.

The gallery surrounds the green as Bobby Jones (right center) putts in the U.S. Amateur.

17

Babe Didrickson Does It All

"Before I was even into my teens, I knew exactly what I wanted to be when I grew up," wrote Babe Didrickson years later. "My goal was to be the greatest athlete that ever lived."

In the 1930s that was a lot to wish for—especially for a woman. But Babe Didrickson came as close to reaching her goal as anyone could hope. In 1950 the sportswriters of the United States almost unanimously named her the greatest woman athlete of the first half-century. The greatest male athlete was Jim Thorpe, and if one had to choose between the two, the choice would be difficult.

Babe Didrickson came to the attention of American sports fans in June 1932. She had already proved to be an amazing athlete in high school at Beaumont, Texas. Her teammates had called her "Babe" after Babe Ruth for the way she could hit a baseball, and she was just as impressive on the school's championship women's basketball team. After high school she went to work for a Dallas insurance company and led the company's AAU women's basketball team to the national title in 1931. But such accomplishments were not widely known.

Now in June 1932 she was competing for the company in the AAU women's track meet at Evanston, Illinois. It was a team competition, but the team from Dallas consisted of one person—Babe Didrickson.

When the two-day meet was over, the Dallas entry had won the team title. The Babe had won the shot put, javelin, long jump, baseball throw and the 80-meter hurdles. She had tied for first in the high jump and taken fourth in the discus. The Illinois Women's Athletic Club, with a team of 22 participants, placed a distant second.

Babe Didrickson poses with a javelin at the 1932 Olympic Games in Los Angeles.

After her amazing performance in Evanston, the Babe suddenly became a top prospect for the women's track and field team at the 1932 Olympic Games, which would be held in Los Angeles. Women's competition had not been added to the Olympic calendar until 1928, so the Babe would be competing in only the second women's games. She seemed disappointed that a special Olympic rule limited her to competing in only three events, but she didn't doubt her ability. "I'm gonna whup 'em all," she promised, and no one accused her of bragging.

On the first day of competition Babe threw the javelin 143 feet, 4 inches, setting

The Babe shows the form that won her gold medals in the hurdles and the javelin throw.

a new world record. This was the first time women's javelin had been included in the Olympics, so of course it was an Olympic record as well. Four days later she set another world record and won another gold medal in the 80-meter hurdles. The new time was 11.7 seconds.

The next day Babe found herself in a fierce battle with teammate Jean Shiley in the high jump. Both competitors cleared 5 feet, 5¼ inches, breaking the old world record. Then in the jump-off for the gold medal, both cleared the bar again.

The Babe had broken three world records in the same week. But this time the judges stepped in to deprive her of her third gold medal. They disqualified her, saying that on the last jump she had "dived" over the bar. So Miss Shiley won the gold. Babe, angry and disappointed because she had

used the same style on the last jump as on all the others, had to settle for the silver.

Despite the last-minute disappointment the Babe's Olympic accomplishments made her the most famous woman athlete of her generation. Shortly after the Olympics she announced that she was taking up golf. Within two years she was shooting in the low 70s and had won the Texas women's championship. By the late 1940s she had become the greatest woman golfer in the world. At one point she won 17 tournaments in a row, which surely must qualify as still another world record.

Basketball, baseball, running, jumping, throwing, golf . . . there seemed no end to the Babe's talents. After the Olympics, writer Paul Gallico asked her, "Is there anything you don't play?"

"Yeah," said Miss Didrickson. "Dolls."

18

Ruth Calls His Shot

In 1932 the New York Yankees were back. They had lost the pennant three straight years to the great Philadelphia Athletics team assembled by manager-owner Connie Mack, the senior statesman of baseball. But if the Yankees had slipped, their superstar Babe Ruth had not. Each of the three Philadelphia years he had led the league in home runs. In 1930, the first Depression year, he set another record by signing a contract for $80,000. Someone asked him if he knew he was being paid more than the President of the United States (Herbert Hoover).

"Well," said the Babe off-handedly, "I had a better year than he did."

Now in 1932 the Yankees had roared to the top of the league, and it was the Babe who was slipping. Although he still hit 41 home runs, he was slower in the field and his pot belly was getting larger. At 37 he was clearly past his prime. Another younger slugger named Jimmy Foxx led the league in homers with 58, and for a few weeks in September it seemed he might break the Babe's record of 60.

Even when the Yanks entered the World Series against a strong Chicago Cub team, Ruth was not his old self. In the first two games he had an error in the field and only two singles at the plate, although the Yanks won both games easily, 12–6 and 5–2.

From the very beginning the two teams had been taunting each other unmercifully, and a special target of the Cubs' abuse was the aging Ruth. Now the Series returned to Chicago for the third game, and the Cubs and their fans had the hated Yanks on home ground. Many fans had come prepared (the pitchers weren't the only ones at Wrigley Field who would be throwing things), and Ruth would be the target of their wrath.

Ruth and Lou Gehrig had put on an awesome show in batting practice before the game. Between them they had slammed 18 "homers" into the distant bleachers. Then in the first inning, with two on, Ruth came to the plate. Cub rooters had brought lemons with them, and hundreds came pelting down at him, along with sizzling insults. From the Cub dugout came a torrent of abuse.

Ruth grinned at the Cubs and waved his bat. Cub pitcher Charley Root threw him two balls. On the next pitch Ruth uncoiled and swung. The ball sailed into the bleachers.

The Babe narrowly missed hitting another homer in the third. By the time he came up in the fifth, the Cubs had tied the game 3–3. Whatever lemons hadn't been hurled at him earlier now flew toward the plate. The hooting and screaming were deafening. "They called me 'big belly' and 'baboon,'" Ruth reported later. The plate umpire glanced nervously at the crowd.

Accounts of what happened next differ slightly, but one account goes like this. Cub fans cheered when Root blazed a called strike. Ruth smiled to the stands and raised one finger, showing the count. Next pitch was a ball. Ruth raised one finger on each hand. The count went to two-and-two, with Ruth making the appropriate signs with his fingers.

Most observers agree that after the last call, Ruth raised his hand and pointed to center field as if to promise that the next ball would go over the fence. The crowd was enraged. The big slugger was mocking them.

On the next pitch Ruth whipped his big bat around, and the ball soared out to center field and over the fence, landing near the flagpole. It hardly seemed possible. Had

After hitting his famous called shot, a smiling Babe Ruth is congratulated by Lou Gehrig.

Ruth really called his shot and then hit the ball over the fence? It certainly seemed that way.

Suddenly there was a change in the Cub crowd. Many who had been booing a moment before were applauding and cheering. In one of baseball's most dramatic moments Ruth had done the impossible—and in the process he had tamed a hostile audience. The next batter was Lou Gehrig, and he hit another homer to assure the Yankee victory. The next day the Yanks smashed the Cubs 13–6 to sweep the Series in four straight games.

The Babe always claimed that he really had pointed to the place where he planned to hit the home run. On the train back to New York he told a sportswriter, "I must be the dumbest man in the world. If I'd missed that homer after calling it, I'd have looked like an awful fool."

Ruth later said that that moment in Chicago was his most satisfying in baseball. It was his last appearance in a World Series, and little more than two years later he retired from baseball. The "called shot" was his last, and certainly his most dramatic, great moment.

19

Jesse Owens at Berlin

It was 3:15 on May 25, 1935. The scene: the Big Ten Track and Field Championships at the University of Michigan in Ann Arbor. The 100-yard dash was about to begin.

The favorite in the race should have been Jesse Owens, the sophomore star from Ohio State. But the week before, Owens had fallen down some stairs and wrenched his back. He hadn't worked out all week, and even on the day of the meet he was in so much pain that he needed help to take off his sweat suit. His coach, Larry Snyder, had even suggested that Jesse withdraw from the 100 yards, since it was only the first of four events that Owens had entered. But Jesse had refused.

Now he was at the starting block. The gun barked, and Owens burst from his mark. In his flawless, fluid style he pulled away from the field to win by five yards. His time, 9.4 seconds, miraculously tied the world record. Owens later said, "When I crouched at the start and the starter said 'get set,' I suddenly forgot the pain."

After the dash Owens went straight to the long jump area. Competition was already underway, and Jesse had agreed with his coach that he would pass up the preliminary jumps and take just one shot, win or lose. He made a couple of short take-off sprints to get his timing right. Then when his turn came he placed a handkerchief in the pit, marking the current world record.

At 3:25 Owens went back to the end of the runway, poised there a second to gain his composure, then sped toward the pit. He made a perfect take-off, and for a long second he seemed to be flying. He landed a full six inches beyond the handkerchief marking the world record! His new record—26 feet, 8¼ inches—would stand for 25 years.

At 3:34, just nine minutes after his amazing jump, Owens lined up for the 220-yard dash. He blazed down the track and won by almost ten yards. His time was 20.3 seconds, still another world record.

By 4:00 attendants had set up the low hurdles along the same 220-yard course, and Jesse Owens was lining up once more. Again he far outdistanced the field, finishing in 22.6 seconds for *another* world mark. In the space of 45 minutes, Jesse Owens had set three world records and tied a fourth.

Jesse came from a poor family in Cleveland and was working his way through Ohio State. Most remarkable to sports fans of the '30s, he was a black man. Few of them could have named another great black athlete be-

Jesse Owens wins a heat in the Big Ten meet. The next day he set four world marks.

cause blacks had been excluded from most other sports. Only in boxing had they gained some recognition. Jesse was the first black college athlete, and the first in track and field, to gain nationwide recognition.

Certainly Jesse's performance at the Big Ten track meet should have been the greatest performance of his life. But there was an even bigger story to come.

The 1936 Olympics were scheduled to be held in Berlin, Germany. In light of this fact, the promise of Jesse Owens took on ominous significance. For in 1933 Adolf Hitler and his Nazi Party had come to power there. Hitler had told the Germans that they belonged to a superior race and that other people, particularly Jews and Negroes, were inferior. As the 1936 Olympics drew nearer, it become obvious that they were being planned to demonstrate German athletic superiority. German papers referred to blacks on the American team as "American Auxiliaries," hinting that they weren't even Americans.

Owens qualified for the Olympics, but it was clear to all that he and the nine other blacks on the U. S. track and field team would be on the spot in Berlin. Many Americans felt that the U. S. team should not even compete in the ugly racist atmosphere in Germany. But the team did go, and Americans uneasily waited to see if Jesse and his black teammates could perform under the pressures and slights they were likely to face.

According to American sportswriters Owens was favored in three individual events: the 100-meter and 200-meter dashes and the long jump. In addition, he would be running one leg for a strong 400-meter relay team. But Adolf Hitler didn't expect him to win any gold medals. Jesse would be competing against the great German sprinter Borschmeyer in the sprints, against German Luz Long in the long jump and against a strong German team in the relay.

Because there were so many entries, Owens had to run four qualifying heats in the 100 meters. The finals came up on a raw, windy day. The thousands of German spectators cheered the husky Borschmeyer as the runners crouched at the start. But when the gun sounded, Jesse Owens pulled away from the field and broke the tape in 10.3 seconds—the fastest 100 meters ever run. It did not become an official world record because the runners had a slight following wind. But the "American Auxiliary" had won a gold medal.

Owens' next event was the long jump. But something was wrong with his form. He fouled on his first attempt to qualify and fouled again on his second attempt. He was in trouble. If he fouled again, he would be disqualified. He stretched out on the grass to relax—and think.

Then the top German jumper, Luz Long,

Owens accelerates in the 200-meter run . . .

came over. Speaking in English, he suggested that Jesse place a marker slightly to the rear of the take-off bar and plan to jump from there to avoid fouling. Jesse followed the advice and qualified easily. Long's gesture was an act of sportsmanship that lightened the grim atmosphere of the Berlin Games for all who observed it.

In the finals Owens jumped just over 26 feet on his second try, setting a new Olympic mark and beating out Luz Long for the gold medal.

The next day Jesse competed in the finals of the 200-meter dash. He had already run three qualifying heats, but when the gun sounded he shot out of the blocks and was soon far ahead of the field. He finished five meters in front with a time of 20.7 seconds, the fastest time ever clocked on a course with one turn.

Two days later Jesse was the lead-off man for the U. S. team in the 400 x 4 sprint relay. The strategy of the American team was to have Owens take a commanding lead and

. . . flies through the air in the long jump and salutes on the victory stand with Luz Long.

let the others try to keep it. Owens handed the second runner a four-meter lead, and the other three Americans held on to win another gold medal. For Jesse, it was his fourth.

The ten black athletes on the U. S. team had all done well. Scored by themselves, they beat the rest of the U. S. team and every other national team in competition. All but one of the ten won at least one medal.

But the man in the spotlight was Jesse Owens. After his second gold medal, the crowd—made up largely of Germans—began a chant that reverberated through the huge stadium: "Jess-see O-wenz . . . Jess-see O-wenz . . . Jess-see O-wenz!"

Hitler's plans to demonstrate racial supremacy had disintegrated, destroyed by the speed and strength of an American black man.

20

Breakthrough for Basketball

Of America's three major sports—baseball, football and basketball—only basketball had not been popular at the turn of the century. And no wonder. Basketball had only been invented in 1891 in Springfield, Massachusetts, by a YMCA instructor named James Naismith.

The game began in a form that fans would

hardly recognize today. It could be played by "any number." The baskets were bushel baskets fastened to poles—there were no backboards. Dribbling was unheard-of, and running with the ball was not allowed, so all movement of the ball had to be accomplished by passing. After every score, teams jumped for the ball at center court. Final scores for games sounded like football scores: 12–10, 19–14, hardly the high totals that would be reached in modern times.

But basketball filled a big need. It was an indoor game for the winter months, something to play or watch between the last football game and the first baseball practice in the spring. Soon high schools and colleges all over the country adopted the game. Dr. Naismith himself was a coach for many years at the University of Kansas.

For some years before 1920, basketball was often played on a court surrounded by wire mesh or net so that the ball could not go out of bounds. The "cage" was hard to keep in repair and even harder on the eyes of spectators, so it was gradually abandoned. But even today basketball players are sometimes still called "cagers."

By the mid-1930s basketball had begun to attract national attention. Several early professional leagues had prospered for a few short years in the 1920s, but "big-time" basketball was played only by the major universities, especially those in the Eastern cities. The sport looked a little more modern —dribbling was part of the game, baskets had backboards and teams were limited to five men.

But scores remained low. There was still a center jump after each basket, and a team averaging 40 points per game was a rarity. A great individual star might average as many as twelve points a game. Teams played a slow, deliberate game, trying to work the ball in close to the basket. If that didn't work, they set up their best outside shooter for a two-handed set shot, which was then considered the only accurate shot from a distance.

Then in the winter of 1935–36 word started trickling across the country from the West that Stanford had something new in basketball. He was a sophomore named Hank Luisetti, and he shot the ball with only one hand!

Conservative coaches smiled. Why did

A drawing of the first basketball game, played in 1892 in Springfield, Massachusetts.

Luisetti's coach let him get away with it? But as Luisetti played out his three varsity years at Stanford, it became harder and harder to laugh at the results he got.

In one game during his sophomore season, Stanford was trailing Southern California by 15 points. They began giving the ball to Luisetti, and the dead-eye forward scored 14 straight points in five minutes.

It wasn't until the next season that the Eastern basketball men got to see Luisetti in action. Stanford came to New York during the Christmas holidays of 1936 to play in Madison Square Garden. They would face Long Island University, the unofficial national champions who had won 43 games in a row.

Sportswriters flocked to a Stanford practice session to see the sharpshooter for themselves. They went away amazed. Luisetti seldom stopped and "set" for a shot. He could fire and score on the dead run. How could anyone stop him?

Long Island tried to stop him and failed. He flashed all over the court, appearing to score almost at will and completely confusing the LIU defense. In the first great basketball upset, Stanford whipped the champs 45–31. Luisetti scored 15.

After the 1936–37 season college rules were changed to eliminate the center jump after every basket. This promised a faster, more wide-open game, but most coaches had not developed a style of play to take advantage of the new rule. Those who were watching Luisetti soon got a clue, however.

Early in the 1937–38 season Stanford met Duquesne University at Cleveland. Luisetti had always been a fine all-around player, taking as much pleasure in a good assist as a good shot. But on this night his teammates were determined that Hank would do the shooting. Every time he threw them a pass, they fired the ball right back.

With no choice but to shoot, Luisetti shot —and scored—from the corners, from the foul circle, from almost every point on the court. Once he slipped and shot from a kneeling position. To the amazement of the Cleveland fans, even that ball went in.

Stanford coach John Bunn took Luisetti out with three minutes left to play. He had scored 23 field goals and 4 freethrows for 50 points! The total shocked basketball—and worried the conservative coaches who still thought the one-hander was a fad. But it soon became clear that Luisetti's new shot was not a fad at all. It was the beginning of a revolution.

Luisetti graduated after becoming the first three-year All-America in basketball. Within a year players all over the country were experimenting with the one-hander. Ten years later the two-handed set shot was nearly extinct, and new "novelties"—the hook and the jump shot—were increasing scoring even more.

But the big step was Luisetti's. He had proved to a skeptical public that in basketball one hand was better than two.

Stanford's Hank Luisetti tries a hook shot.

21

Joe Louis' Revenge

On the night of June 22, 1938, Yankee Stadium in New York was jammed for the most dramatic heavyweight championship fight of the decade. The champ, Joe Louis, was entering the ring. As he came down the aisle, fans screamed at him from all sides.

"You gotta do it for the U.S.A., Joe!"

"Knock him cold, Joe . . . Adolf Hitler sent him!"

Joe Louis was facing Max Schmeling, the champion of Adolf Hitler's Germany. And, like Jesse Owens, Louis was black, making him particularly sensitive to Hitler's belief that black men were naturally inferior.

Owens had won his gold medals in Nazi Berlin in 1936. Now, two years later, few men could doubt Hitler's intention of taking control of all Europe. He had frightened Austria into accepting Nazi rule and had invaded Czechoslovakia. "Today Germany —tomorrow the world!" he had declared. Already Americans were lining up against the aggression and bigotry that Hitler represented.

But Joe Louis also had something personal to prove. Two years earlier Joe had faced this same Max Schmeling—and he had lost, much to the pleasure of the Nazi Party. So Joe had a score to settle for his race, and for himself.

In 1934 and 1935, young Joe Louis had rocketed to boxing fame with a succession of knockout victories. He was then the most exciting young heavyweight in years, and he was already planning to fight champion Jimmy Braddock. But first he was matched with Schmeling, the European champion, for a bout on June 18, 1936. Joe's fans thought that Schmeling would be a good tune-up—lasting perhaps six rounds against Joe's amazing power and speed.

Tough Max Schmeling had other ideas. Early in the fight he noticed that when Joe threw his right, he dropped his left a bit. Schmeling craftily came in over the lowered left with his own hard right.

Louis never understood what was happening. After six rounds he was in serious trouble. The devastating Bomber from Detroit was bombing out. Ringsiders and a nationwide radio audience were stunned. Finally, in the tenth round, Schmeling knocked Louis out.

Max Schmeling returned to Germany

An exultant Max Schmeling watches as Joe Louis is counted out in 1936.

Two years after their first fight, Schmeling falls to Joe's vicious first-round attack.

scornful of the man he had beaten. "He fought like an amateur," the German sneered. "This is no man who could ever be champion."

Joe Louis heard about Schmeling's comment. He brooded and said little, nursing his wounds and his pride. Back on the championship trail again, he added new victims to his knockout record and got his match with Jimmy Braddock, the champion. Louis made easy work of Braddock, knocking him out in the eighth round, and became heavyweight champion of the world.

He had fame, wealth and everything that goes with the heavyweight crown. But there was one thing Joe Louis still wanted—a return bout with Max Schmeling.

American fans were eager for the fight, but few people, aside from his manager, Jack Blackburn, knew how savagely eager Louis was for the rematch. So on June 22, 1938, exactly a year after he had won the title from Braddock, Joe Louis was giving Max Schmeling a crack at his crown.

One wonders whether Joe Louis even heard the fans shouting encouragement as he climbed into the ring at Yankee Stadium. He already knew that Schmeling had promised Chancellor Hitler he would take the title

from the black man and bring it back to Germany. Joe stared coldly across the ring at Schmeling. His face showed no emotion when the referee called the two fighters to the center of the ring.

At the bell, Louis glided swiftly out of his corner, stalking the confident Schmeling. Schmeling was waiting for Louis to drop his left hand as he had done in the first fight, leaving himself open for Schmeling's counter punch.

But suddenly Louis' left jab flashed out twice, rapidly, jolting Schmeling's head back. A few seconds later Louis landed a thudding right to the jaw and drove Schmeling against the ropes with rights and lefts to the head and body. Joe caught the German with a left hook, a right cross, then another hook and a right that sent Schmeling tumbling to the canvas for a count of three.

The crowd roared, sensing the kill, as Schmeling got up and Louis swiftly pursued him. Two lefts and another crunching right sent Schmeling reeling. Then Louis thundered another right into his side, near the kidney. Schmeling went down, and ringsiders later said that even above the roar of the crowd they had heard Schmeling scream after the last right-hand punch.

Somehow Schmeling got up, only to have Louis blast him with a left hook and a right cross to the jaw. Max Schmeling fell face down and lay motionless.

When referee Arthur Donovan had counted Schmeling out, only two minutes and four seconds had passed in the first round. In two minutes Joe Louis had taken his revenge on the man who had sneered at him and insulted his whole race.

The roar from the fans was unbelievable. Radio announcers were in a frenzy to get to Louis in the ring. But no emotion showed on Joe Louis' face. He had known what he had to do—and he had done it. The world of boxing had never known such vengeful moments as the two minutes it took Joe Louis to destroy Max Schmeling.

22

Gehrig's Farewell

One afternoon in May 1939 the newspapers and radio broadcasts carried a startling bulletin: "Lou Gehrig did not play." All over the country baseball fans talked about the report. An aide made a special point to give the news to President Roosevelt.

That afternoon, the New York Yankees had played in Detroit. Before the game their captain and first baseman, Lou Gehrig, handed the batting order to the umpire. Listed at first base was Babe Dahlgren. Then Gehrig went back to the dugout. In the bottom of the first, when the Yankees took the field, Lou Gehrig stayed on the bench, and the news went out to the country: Gehrig is out.

What was so remarkable about a baseball player taking a day off? Lou Gehrig had not missed a playing day since June 2, 1925. He had played in 2,130 consecutive major league games, a figure so far beyond other players that it was ridiculous. For nearly 14 seasons, Lou had shrugged off ailments that would have kept lesser men home in bed—spike wounds, perforated blisters, fever, headaches, sore throats. Long before he sat out that game in Detroit, Gehrig was known as the "Iron Horse."

And Gehrig was no ordinary player. Fans could point to only a handful of others who had equaled or surpassed his level of performance: Ty Cobb, Babe Ruth, Honus Wagner, perhaps . . . the list was a short one. In his long career he had hit 493 home runs, then second only to Babe Ruth. He had driven in 1,990 runs, also second to Ruth, and three times he had driven in more than 170 runs in a single season. He had a glittering lifetime batting average of .340. And he was a great first baseman. All this without missing a single game in 14 years.

Lou Gehrig, baseball's Iron Horse.

Gehrig was only 35 years old, but there had been signs even in 1938 that he was slowing down. He had been ill on and off, but doctors could not decide what the trouble was. In spring training before the 1939 season his coordination had seemed to be a little off, but Gehrig kept working to get into shape and get his batting eye back. Then in the first eight games of the regular season he got only four singles in 28 times at bat for a miserable .148 average. This was not the Lou Gehrig the fans had loved for so many years.

Gehrig bows his head as Yankee fans and players honor him on Lou Gehrig Day.

So on May 2, Gehrig took himself out of the line-up. "I made the decision last Sunday," he told reporters after the game. "I just haven't helped the club. I don't want to keep coming up with men on base and not do anything about it. The last four times I've been up, there were men on base . . ." He shook his head sadly.

Yankee manager Joe McCarthy had mixed feelings. "I'm sorry to see it happen. Players and men like him come along once in a hundred years," he said. Then he added, "We'll miss him, but I think he's doing the proper thing."

Within weeks it became known that Gehrig was suffering from a rare progressive disease called amyotrophic lateral sclerosis. It was incurable, and it would soon kill him. On July 4, 1939, the Yankees organized a "Lou Gehrig Day" at Yankee Stadium. Gehrig came to the microphone at home plate after being honored by his past and present teammates and told the 61,000 fans,

"You've been reading about my tough breaks for weeks now. But today I think I'm the luckiest man alive. I feel more than ever that I have much to live for . . ."

The Iron Horse was close to emotional collapse. Babe Ruth, who had left the Yankees four years earlier, threw his arms around Lou in a huge bear hug, and many in the crowd and on the field were in tears. It was a hard way for a great athlete to go out.

Gehrig turned in his Yankee uniform and did part-time youth work for the City of New York. Less than two years later he died.

The decade was drawing to a close. The nation—and sports—had survived the Great Depression. But just as it seemed that sport was ready to take off on another boom, history took one of its wayward steps. On September 1, 1939, Adolf Hitler's Nazi legions invaded Poland and the nations of Europe declared war. Soon the war would engulf the United States as well.

PART V
1940-1949

As the new decade dawned, America was already preparing for war, although many still hoped (as in 1915 and 1916) that she could stay out of it. The years 1940 and 1941 were increasingly prosperous for Americans, but the news from overseas got grimmer every day. In 1940 France and the low countries were overrun by the Nazi armies of Germany and another front was opened when the Nazis suddenly invaded Russia. In the East, Japanese armies threatened all of China and Southeast Asia. Americans began supplying British armies with equipment and weapons. The U. S. Army began to draft men—just in case—but officially, the nation was still at peace.

The end of peace came with suddenness and shock on December 7, 1941. Early that Sunday morning the Japanese attacked Pearl Harbor, a big American navy base in Hawaii. Thousands of American sailors died as their ships were exploded and sunk right in the harbor. Every American who was old enough to understand can remember where he was and what he was doing when he heard the news. The following day Congress declared war, and for the next three and a half years most of the country's energy went into the war effort.

Millions of young men enlisted or were drafted into the service. They were sent to fight in Italy, the South Pacific and later in France and Germany. Some women also enlisted and served in the military, and millions of others went to work in defense industries. "Rosie the Riveter," who helped assemble ships, tanks and airplanes, became a symbol of women's new freedom and responsibility. There were shortages of rubber, gasoline and many kinds of food, and people at home learned to make do with whatever was available. The news was filled with battle reports from far-away places.

America's entry into the war proved to be decisive. The war in Europe

The disaster at Pearl Harbor sends the United States to war . . . General Eisenhower talks to the troops . . . and young Frank Sinatra croons as his teenage audience swoons.

ended with the surrender of Germany in April 1945. In July the United States dropped the first atomic bombs on Hiroshima and Nagasaki, Japan. Within days of the second bomb, Japan surrendered as well. The U. S. suffered far less than other countries, but there were thousands of casualties nonetheless.

Meanwhile, hand in hand with the fighting came major scientific discoveries: penicillin, DDT, radar—and the splitting of the atom, which led to the terrifying atom bomb.

After the war America experienced a boom. During the war years there hadn't been much to buy, so people had saved their money. Afterward they earned more and spent it at new record levels for homes, cars, appliances and leisure time activities. By 1949 television was the big topic of conversation— the newest of the communications wonders.

Like other activities, sport prospered in 1940 and 1941, slowed down during the war years and saw an unparalleled boom afterward. Baseball reached its greatest popularity in the late '40s, attracting thousands of fans with more and more night games. College football followed close behind. The National Basketball Association was formed in 1948 with teams in such places as Fort Wayne, Syracuse, Tri-Cities and Sheboygan as well as New York, Boston and Philadelphia. But it would be years before many sports fans would consider pro basketball a big-time attraction.

In 1948 the Olympics, which had been interrupted by war, were held for the first time since 1936. Joe Louis came back from wartime service to claim his crown and reigned until 1949. Tennis saw the advent of two new champions—Jack Kramer and Pancho Gonzales—and golf was dominated by a little giant named Ben Hogan.

But as the 1940s began, America was still at peace. And our biggest battle of the year took place on a football field.

81

23

Victory for the T

In 1940 George Halas' Chicago Bears surprised the National Football League with a new formation—the T. The T wasn't really new. It had been part of football in the early 1900s. But until 1940 football's standard formations had been the single wing, the double wing and the old Notre Dame shift.

Halas, the founder, owner and coach of the Bears, revived the T and gave it a new look. The Bears' quarterback set up directly behind the center. In back of him were the fullback and two halfbacks in a line parallel to the line of scrimmage. Halas was the first

Quarterback Sid Luckman and coach George Halas on the bench during the title game.

to see possibilities for deception in the T, and during the 1940 season he began putting those possibilities into practice.

The Bears had a good season, losing only three games. One reason for their success was the fact that the other pro teams didn't quite know how to defense the new formation. Still, there was no real panic—some other teams were doing almost as well without the T. But on December 8, 1940, pro football got the word: the T formation was definitely worth panicking about.

The Bears were playing the Washington Redskins for the NFL championship that day. The Skins were a super team, featuring pro football's first great passer, Slingin' Sammy Baugh, who completed an amazing 60 percent of his passes. Only three weeks earlier in a regular season game, the Skins had beat the Bears 7–3 in a tightly contested game, so they were slightly favored to win the NFL title.

But the Bears weren't exactly pushovers. For a start, they had rookie quarterback Sid Luckman, a slick passer and ball-handler. But what Halas liked most about Luckman was his brains. Halas had brought Luckman from Columbia, where he had been a single-wing tailback, and taught him nearly 200 plays that could be run off the T—more than any previous coach had thought possible or necessary. And the Bears had more than just Luckman. George McAfee was a great halfback, Bill Osmanski a crunching fullback. And Joe Stydahar at tackle, Danny Fortmann at guard and Bulldog Turner at center were the league's best.

Now on this crisp, December day in Washington, D.C., before 30,000 fans, the Bears were hoping for more than a championship. They wanted two other

Chicago back Bill Osmanski outruns the Washington defenders for long yardage.

things: to prove the T would really work and to get revenge for their recent loss to Washington.

Halas wasn't the only man working on the T. In preparation for the championship game he had gotten the help of Clark Shaughnessy, the coach at Stanford University. Together, the two had planned a couple of new wrinkles to try out against the Skins.

The Bears wasted no time. On their first play from scrimmage they ran to the left. Then on the second play McAfee went into motion to the left. Luckman took the snap, faked a handoff to running back Ray Nolting, who was following McAfee, then gave the ball to Osmanski, the fullback. Osmanski cracked over left tackle, found a big hole, swerved to the outside and with the help of a spectacular block, raced 68 yards for a touchdown.

On their second series of downs the Bears unveiled a new trick. They put a man in motion to the left to draw the defense to that side. Then they sent the ball-carrier to the

right. This "counter" play completely disorganized the Redskins, and Chicago scored again on a long 17-play drive. At the end of the first quarter the Bears led 21–0, and at halftime it was 28–0. Now the sportswriters began to exchange glances. The T was working flawlessly.

The Redskins wanted desperately to get back into the game in the second half. But on their second play, Baugh's pass was intercepted and returned for a touchdown. Now, flashing out of a variation of their T, the Bears ripped the Redskins to pieces. By the end of the third period the score was 54–0. Washington players came out of the game with tears of frustration running down their faces.

In the fourth quarter the Bears tallied their *tenth* touchdown. The referee asked Halas to please run or pass for extra points from then on because there was only one football left. Those kicked into the stands for extra points had been kept by the fans.

The final, unbelievable score was 73–0. For a pro championship game! With the new T formation—not to mention the great Chicago defense—the Bears had gained 372 yards rushing to the Redskins three.

Many football experts—including George Halas—believe this game had a greater effect on football than any other single game ever played. "The way the Bears murdered the Skins brought attention to the T formation as nothing else could do," said Halas.

By the end of the 1940s there was hardly a major team in football that used anything but the T. There would be many refinements, but from that day to this, the T has been the winning formation in the game.

24

A Streak for Jolting Joe

It caused no great stir around the country when Joe DiMaggio, center fielder for the New York Yankees, got a single in four times at bat against the White Sox on May 15, 1941. Nor was any particular notice paid the next day when he belted out a triple and a home run. The next week reporters mentioned casually that the Yankee Clipper, as DiMaggio was called, had hit safely in his seventh straight game.

Soon the American public was listening eagerly every night to the radio news. There were grim reports from Europe: France had already fallen to the German armies, and England was expecting to be invaded. But many listeners were more interested in the big sports news—the hitting streak of 26-year-old Joe DiMaggio. On June 3, Joe got a single against Detroit—20 straight games; on June 10, a single against Chicago—25 straight!

The pressure began to mount. Joe was already a top baseball hero, but with the whole country following his every game, his nerves would have to be as steady as his bat. Official scorers around the league began to feel the pressure, too. In close situations, they had to decide whether Joe had really gotten a hit or reached base on an error. What if the hitting streak was ended by a bad call—or even worse, what if fans began to suspect that DiMaggio was getting special favors from the men with the score pads?

Fans were now flocking to ball parks. Some hoped to see their own pitchers end DiMaggio's streak; others hoped to see Joe extend it. Either way, everyone wanted to be in on baseball history.

On June 20, Joe tied Rogers Hornsby's National League mark by hitting in 33 straight games. On June 28, he stroked a single and double against Philadelphia to tie George Sisler's major league mark of 41. And the next day he set a new record of 42 with a single against Washington.

The graceful DiMaggio seemed cool and

Joe DiMaggio gets a single against Washington, bringing his streak to 42 games.

unruffled—and he could do nothing wrong at the plate. At least once in every game he banged the ball past fielders and arrived safely at first (or second or third). Now the increasingly excited fans began to wonder how long he could continue. Some dreamers thought Joe might go on forever.

On July 2, DiMaggio slammed a homer against the Red Sox, making it 45 games in a row. On July 11, he made it 50 with a homer and three singles against the St. Louis Browns.

The streak had to end, of course. And as with most streaks, the moment the fans remembered was the day it ended. On July 17, more than two months after the streak started, 67,468 fans came out to a night game in Cleveland. The day before Joe had gotten three hits for his 56th straight game.

Now Joe was facing Indian ace, lefty Al Smith. His first time up he hit a screaming bounder down the foul line. Indian third baseman Ken Keltner made a brilliant stop and threw DiMaggio out. On Joe's next trip to the plate, Smith walked him. Half the crowd groaned; the other half cheered.

His next time up DiMaggio slashed another hot grounder down third. Keltner lunged and made another spectacular catch, then threw across the diamond to first. Joe was out again.

In the eighth inning, with a man on first, the Clipper faced relief pitcher Jim Bagby, a right-handed knuckle-baller. Unless the game went to extra innings, this would be Joe's last chance to keep his streak alive. Joe unleashed his bat and hit a crazily bounding ground ball deep to short. Lou Boudreau, Cleveland's slick player-manager, fielded the ball and turned it into a double play. Baseball's longest major league hitting streak was over at 56 games.

Joe had gone more than two months without a hitless game, breaking the old major league record by 15. During the streak he had batted at a .408 clip, getting 91 hits including 15 homers, and driving in 55 runs.

Years later sportswriters agreed that the streak was baseball's most unapproachable record, unlikely to ever be equaled.

Through all the excitement about DiMaggio's hitting streak, many fans had failed to notice that Ted Williams, the young slugger of the Boston Red Sox, was hitting over .400. But after July 17, Williams began to get the attention. No one had batted .400 all season since 1930. But if anyone could do it, Williams could. The skinny young man was only 22 years old, but he had made a lifetime study of hitting.

Going into September Ted's average was .413. But as the season neared its end, the pressure began to tell. His average fell closer and closer to .400. On the final day of the season, with a doubleheader still to play, he was batting .3995. Since the average would be rounded off to .400, Williams could preserve his position by sitting out the last two games. The pennant race had already been decided, so his manager offered to let him sit it out.

Ted Williams shakes hands with DiMaggio (5) after winning the 1941 All-Star game.

But Williams didn't want to back into the great accomplishment. He insisted on playing. And in eight official at-bats that day, he got six hits and brought his average to .406. It was a splendid performance under pressure.

Just over two months later, the Japanese attacked Pearl Harbor and the country went to war. Ted Williams and Joe DiMaggio disappeared from baseball along with hundreds of lesser-known players to serve in the armed forces. In their places during the war years played men too old or too young for the draft and those who were exempted because of injury or hardship. The nation still followed baseball, but the quality of play suffered. Williams and DiMaggio did come back in 1946, however, to continue their long competition.

In all the years that followed, baseball records fell and new records were set. But two that seemed likely to last forever were Williams' .400 season and Joe DiMaggio's amazing 56-game hitting streak.

25

The Rocket's Goal-a-Game

One night the Montreal Canadiens were playing an exhibition game against a minor league hockey team in Johnstown, Pennsylvania. It was clearly a mismatch, and someone suggested to the Canadiens that they take it easy against the local club. Canadien star Maurice "Rocket" Richard (pronounced Ree-SHARD) didn't seem to understand—he went out and tallied seven goals in one period.

"You have to understand," he explained later. "I can only play hockey one way. The hard way."

Richard played for the Canadiens from 1943 to 1960, and during those years he became the greatest star in hockey history.

Rocket Richard scores against Boston Bruin goalie Red Henry in a 1953 playoff game.

The fans in Montreal loved him—not only because he was a remarkable player, but because he was a French-Canadian who represented the people of French-speaking Quebec province in a unique way. Unfortunately, his countrymen's enthusiasm for Richard sometimes got out of hand. In 1955, when the president of the National Hockey League suspended Richard for hitting an official, the Montreal fans staged the worst sports riot in North American history. They threatened the president and smashed windows in a 15-block stretch of Montreal.

Richard had thousands of fans in the United States as well. They weren't inclined to riot in his favor, but they did grant that Rocket Richard was probably the most exciting competitor who ever put on skates.

Richard had been a machinist as a youth. But there was no way the machinist's trade would be his career. He had already shown that he could skate and shoot a hockey puck like no other player in Canada. The Canadiens signed him in 1942 when he was 20. He had already broken so many bones that he couldn't qualify for military duty anyway. He played for the Canadiens from the start, and halfway through his first pro season (1942–43) he broke an ankle. Early in his second season he cracked his shoulder, and he missed a few games but wound up scoring 32 goals.

That set the stage for his greatest accomplishment. In 1944–45 the Rocket was ready to take off. He scored his first goal in the third game. In his fifth he turned his first hat trick with three goals. About a week later he slashed another hat trick into the records. He now had 12 goals in 13 games. The word was racing around the league that this French-Canadian who played an aggressive, even wild, game might break the scoring record. Since the NHL was established in its modern form in 1926, no one had ever averaged a goal a game, and no one had scored more than 43 goals in a season. Yet here was a player in his first full NHL season who was threatening both marks.

Young Richard in his rookie season with the Montreal Canadiens.

Richard shot left-handed, yet he played right wing. His skating style and unorthodox stickhandling baffled the defenders. But as he racked up goal after goal he began receiving brutal attention from defensemen, getting bodychecked legally and illegally. He was slashed, high-sticked and needlessly slammed into the boards. His blood was splattered on every rink in the league. Other young players might have been intimidated, but not Richard. He continued his goal-a-game rate, and in one contest he scored five goals to go way ahead of the pace.

In his 40th game Richard got his 44th goal, breaking the modern NHL record. Defenses became more desperate than ever as headlines announced the possibility of the Rocket hitting 50-for-50. In the next nine games his opponents kept him to just five goals. Going into the 50th and final game, Richard had 49 goals. The game was broadcast throughout Canada, and Canadian troops in Europe demanded Richard hockey bulletins with their rations.

The game was against the Boston Bruins, and before the evening was over word went out that the Rocket had succeeded. In a 4–1 victory he had scored his 50th goal in the 50th and last game of the season.

Over the years, great scorers came and went, and scoring became easier as the game expanded. But no one—not Gordie Howe or Bobby Hull or even Phil Esposito—ever matched the Rocket's goal-a-game pace.

26

A Black Man for Baseball

On April 27, 1946, the eyes of the sports world turned to an unlikely place—a baseball stadium in Jersey City, New Jersey, just across the Hudson River from New York. On that day the Jersey City Giants would be facing the Montreal Royals in the opening game of the season for the International League.

What could be so interesting about a

Jackie Robinson in 1946, a week before his first game in organized baseball.

minor league game? And how could the minors provide a great moment in sport?

The answer lay in the story of Jackie Robinson, a 27-year-old rookie on the Montreal roster. Most reports agreed that he was a promising infielder, a fine hitter and a speedy baserunner. But it wasn't his arms and legs that people talked about—it was his skin. Jackie Robinson was a black man.

For 50 years the major and minor leagues that made up "organized baseball" had used only white players. There was no law against blacks, but custom and an unwritten agreement between team owners had kept them out. After all, there were separate black teams and leagues that played for black audiences. Some whites in baseball didn't understand why "they" should want to play with "us."

The separation of the races was not limited to baseball. In the South, hotels, schools and restaurants were segregated by law. And in the rest of the country, unwritten laws prevented blacks from living in many neighborhoods and applying for many jobs.

But times were changing. In baseball there had been talk of admitting blacks for several years. Some teams had even had tryouts for promising black players. Still, no one seemed willing to risk the anger of white players and fans by actually signing a black man to a contract and putting him on the field.

Then late in 1945 Branch Rickey, general

manager of the National League's Brooklyn Dodgers, met with Jackie Robinson. He told Robinson that he was determined to break the color line in baseball and that he wanted Jackie to be the first black player.

Robinson had been the greatest all-around athlete in the history of UCLA in 1938–40. He was an All-America running back in football and a star on the baseball, basketball and track teams. During World War II he had served in the Army (which was still largely segregated) and had forced the Army to admit him and other blacks to Officers' Candidate School. He had been playing shortstop for the black Kansas City Monarchs when Rickey's scouts discovered him.

Rickey warned Robinson that being the first black would be a tense and perhaps even dangerous job. Jackie would have to suppress his combative instincts for a while and learn to ignore insults, beanballs and intentional roughness. "I want a man who has the guts *not* to fight back!" Rickey told him.

Rickey announced that Robinson had been signed in December 1945. From then on, the sports world watched his progress and waited to see him in action. The young shortstop got off to a shaky start. In spring training he was troubled with a sore arm and had to learn to play first base. Several racial incidents marred his stay at the Dodger camp in Florida. Nevertheless, he was assigned for the 1946 season to Montreal, the Dodgers' top farm team. When the Royals moved North, newspapers all over the country prepared to cover his first game in Jersey City.

The stadium was packed with people—not only Jersey City fans but also Jackie Robinson fans. When he came to bat in the top of the first, he was cheered by thousands, many of them black people who had come to see his first appearance. The nervous rookie grounded out to the shortstop. In the bottom of the first, a hard-hit ball skittered past him into right field for a Jersey City hit. Robinson might have had a chance at it, but he was having trouble concentrating.

Could he succeed? Would he advance the cause of integrating baseball or set it back? That was the question on many people's minds. They didn't have to wait long for a hint of the answer.

In the third inning Jackie came up with two men on. By this time he had settled down, and when he got a good pitch he blasted it deep to left field. As he approached first base, he could tell it was a home run by the cheers from the stands. Three runs scored for Montreal.

Robinson is congratulated by a teammate after his third-inning home run.

As a Brooklyn Dodger star in 1949, Robinson steals home against the Chicago Cubs.

A few innings later Robinson singled. Branch Rickey had urged Robinson to avoid fighting back against insults, but he had also urged Robinson to play the game aggressively. So right away Jackie began dancing off first, threatening to steal second base. The pitcher tried to pick him off and failed. Then on the first pitch Jackie streaked toward second, beating the catcher's throw. Moments later he took third on a grounder to the third baseman. Runners don't usually advance in this situation, but the moment the third baseman let go of the ball, Jackie was on his way. Again he beat the throw.

Even on third, Robinson would not be satisfied. He took a long lead, turned as if to go back to the bag, then dashed part way toward home as the pitcher released his pitch. The poor Jersey City hurler was so unnerved that on the next pitch he balked, giving Robinson a free walk home.

By this time the crowd was unanimously cheering Robinson. He was playing for the visiting team and he was black, but everyone could appreciate the daring, resourceful kind of baseball he played.

The game turned into a rout as Montreal won 14–2. Rookie Jackie Robinson had four hits, including a home run, in five times at bat. He had driven in four runs and scored four—one when he got a second Jersey City pitcher to balk.

That may have been the most important game in Robinson's career, but it was only the first of many sparkling performances. He helped Montreal win the International League pennant that year and was the hero in their Little World Series victory after the regular season. In April 1947 he made his debut with the Brooklyn Dodgers, becoming the first black man to play major league ball in modern times. His first game with the Dodgers was hardly spectacular—he went hitless in three at-bats—but by the end of the season his new team had won a pennant and Robinson had won National League Rookie of the Year honors. Two years later he was voted Most Valuable Player.

By the time Robinson retired in 1957, black players had become common in organized baseball. The best of them—Willie Mays and Hank Aaron, for instance—were among the great stars of the game. But every black ballplayer could look back on Robinson's early performances with pride and gratitude. By meeting the challenge of being first, he had made it easier for all who followed.

27

The Youngest Olympic Hero

In the autumn of 1944 a thin, awkward freshman named Robert Mathias was playing the trumpet in the Tulare (California) High School band at football games. Underweight and anemic, he didn't seem to be cut out for sports.

Four years later, in August of 1948, Robert Mathias was on the field at Wembley Stadium in London, England. Wembley was the scene of the 1948 Olympics, and Mathias was not there as a trumpet player. He was there to compete in the decathlon, the medley of ten events that determines who is the world's greatest all-around athlete. Mathias was 17 years old, the youngest athlete in the history of the U. S. track and field team.

In those four years the scrawny trumpet player had clearly come a long way. Bob Mathias had always been interested in sports, but he'd grown too quickly and was weak and anemic. His father, a doctor who had played football at Oklahoma, began to build his son up with vitamins and diet. And by his junior year in high school Bob was 6-foot-2, weighed 190 pounds and was a star in varsity football, basketball and track. As a senior he was one of the top athletes in California.

Late in Bob's senior year his coach, Virgil Jackson, suggested that Bob consider the decathlon. With his versatility and strength he might do well. With diligent training he might even qualify for the 1952 Olympics in another four years. Bob liked the idea, but he saw no reason to wait that long. There would be an Olympics that very summer.

The Olympic regional decathlon meet was only three weeks away. Mathias had never run a distance event in his life, and the decathlon called for the 400 and 1500 meters. Bob had never pole-vaulted either—or long-jumped, put the shot or thrown a javelin. He had run sprints, hurdled and thrown a discus. But in three weeks he would have to learn the mechanics of several new events.

At the regional meet Bob Mathias won the decathlon with 7,094 points. Track and field followers couldn't believe it. A couple of weeks later at the national meet in Bloomfield, New Jersey, the top three finishers would qualify for the 1948 Olympic team. Mathias scored a sensational 7,244 points there to place first. Soon after, he sailed for London.

Foreign stars at Wembley weren't impressed by the stories they heard about Mathias. The decathlon was an event where experience counted. An athlete had to learn to pace himself, saving enough energy to do well in each of the ten events. The scoring system gave equal weight to each event, awarding bonus points for excellent performances and penalizing a contestant for any performance below a certain standard. Athletes who tired too quickly would lose ground in the later events.

August 5, the first day of the decathlon, was gloomy and drizzling. The decathlon performers would be on the field for almost twelve hours that day, completing five of the ten events.

In his first event Mathias ran a respectable 100 meters. Then he took third place in the long jump, with 21 feet, 8½ inches. In the shot put he was elated when he got off a good one but perplexed when he saw the red foul flag go up.

"After your throw you left the ring by

Young Bob Mathias competes in four of ten decathlon events at the 1948 Olympics: the 100-meter dash, the long jump, the high jump and the 110-meter hurdles.

way of the front half," the official explained. "You must exit by the rear half."

Mathias' next throw wasn't quite as good.

He ran a fine 51.7 for the 400 meters, then went into the day's last event, the high jump. He was trailing several of the other competitors and would have to do well to stay close to them. To do that he needed a jump of at least six feet.

With the bar at 5-foot-9 he failed his first two efforts. Before his final try he sat on the wet grass, huddled in a blanket, thinking. Then he made a desperate decision. He would abandon his Western roll technique and rely on his natural strength and coordination. It was risky to change his form at the last minute, but Mathias felt it was his only chance.

He took a deep breath and sprinted at the bar, straight on. On take-off he used all the power in his body, going up awkwardly and off-balance. Then he was over the bar. Mathias went on to a fine leap of 6 feet, 1¼ inches and ended the day in third place, trailing Kistenmacher of Argentina by 51 points and Heinrich of France by 32.

A few minutes later Kistenmacher met Bob in the locker room. He showed him a score card of the events and said there was no way Mathias could catch up in the second day of competition. The young American

suggested they compare notes again in 24 hours.

The next morning the weather was terrible: raw, rainy and foggy. The decathlon events were put off until the afternoon. Then Mathias ran the first event, the 110-meter hurdles, in 15.7, keeping him even with the leaders. Next was the discus, one of his best events. Showing good form, he went into his whirl and put all his strength into the throw. The disk flew 144 feet, 4 inches—the best mark in the event by far. He had passed Kistenmacher and Heinrich to take the lead for the first time.

Now it was almost 9:00 P.M., and there were still three events to go. Mathias had eaten a box lunch in the afternoon, but he had been too tired to eat at dinner time. The next event was the pole vault. It was now dark, and since Wembley Stadium had no lights, the contestants would have to race down a darkened path toward a bar illuminated by a few powerful flashlights.

To save his strength, Mathias passed up the preliminary jumps until the bar reached ten feet. It was a risky strategy. If he failed at ten feet he would be penalized and lose all chance of winning a medal. On his first try he swung up on the pole toward the barely visible crossbar. He seemed to hang in the air for an instant, then came down in

the pit without disturbing the crossbar. Later he cleared 11 feet, 5¾ inches to win the event and extend his lead.

Now there were two events left: the javelin throw and the 1,500-meter run. After eight events Mathias had a comfortable lead, but he was nearing exhaustion. To make things more difficult, the 1,500 meters was his worst event. That meant his javelin throw would have to be really good.

The javelin was slippery and hard to grasp in the rain. And in the dark stadium a contestant could not even follow its flight. Even the most experienced competitors would have trouble overcoming these hazards. But how would Mathias manage? Until three months ago he had never held a javelin in his hand.

Two officials held flashlights at the foul line. Bob broke into his loping run, approached the line and flung the long spear. It soared up and out, landing in the soggy turf at 165 feet, 1 inch. He had won another event and lengthened his lead in the point totals.

Now there was just the tortuous 1,500 meters left. It was almost 11:00 P.M. Mathias needed a time under 5 minutes, 30 seconds to become the decathlon champion.

World record time in the event was well under four minutes, so 5:30 seemed to be an easy time. But after being pounded all day by runners and rain the track was in terrible shape. And the young athlete who had run nine punishing events in 36 hours was nearing the limits of his endurance. He pushed on through the fog and rain, giving everything he had as a handful of Americans screamed encouragement from the dark stands. As Mathias came around the final turn he called on his muscles for one last effort—and they responded. He crossed the finish line in 5:11.

Bob Mathias was the Olympic decathlon champion with 7,139 points. At 17, he was the world's greatest athlete and the youngest ever to win a gold medal in Olympic track and field.

After the Olympics Bob entered Stanford University and became an All-America football player. In 1949 and 1950 he again won the national decathlon title. Then in 1952 he announced that he would try to become the first man to win a second Olympic gold medal in the grueling event. In Helsinki, Finland, he overwhelmed the field to win by a margin of more than 900 points over the second place finisher.

In following years the United States would produce other great decathlon champions. But none would surpass the amazing performance of young Bob Mathias.

Rock & roll idol Elvis Presley . . . an early television set . . . and Russia's Sputnik, prophet of the space age.

PART VI

1950-1959

As the 1950s dawned, the United States was more prosperous than ever before. World War II had been over for nearly five years, and most people looked forward to long years of peace.

But America was now the greatest world power and would find it hard not to be drawn into any military dispute on the globe. The United Nations, formed at the end of World War II, supposedly gave all countries a chance to settle their disputes peacefully. But in reality the world had broken into two hostile camps. The Soviet Union led the Communist bloc, and the U.S. led the so-called Free World.

In June 1950 dreams of peace were shattered once again. The troops of North Korea, a Communist nation supported by Russia and mainland China, invaded South Korea, an ally of the United States. At American urging, the United Nations took the side of South Korea and sent UN troops (90 percent of them American) to repel the invasion.

In 1952 General Dwight Eisenhower was elected President. In his first year he brought the fighting in Korea to an end through negotiation, and the rest of the decade was largely peaceful and quiet.

There were some quiet revolutions going on, however. In Russia, scientists were working on a rocket that could put a small satellite in orbit around the earth. In 1957 they launched the Sputnik into earth orbit. Americans were amazed, and the government began a crash program to match the Soviet accomplishment.

Closer to home, a revolution was brewing in music. It was called rock & roll, and it gained a generation of young fans. The most famous rock & roller was Elvis Presley, whose sullen good looks, duck-tail haircut and rhythmic gyrations set his fans screaming with delight—and their parents screaming with outrage.

But the biggest revolution of all was television. Since the 1920s movies and radio had been the popular entertainers of the nation. But now they were eclipsed as TV entered almost every American home. Spindly antennas became a common sight on the roofs of mansions and shacks alike. TV brought new attractions both for young viewers and grown-ups: cowboys, comedians, variety shows, political events and serious drama.

94

Television also brought big changes to sport. Most important, it brought professional football to the very top of sports popularity. The pros had struggled for years, but with TV coverage they were soon the most prosperous people in sport. TV was a mixed blessing for baseball, however. Although it brought major league games to millions who had never seen them before, it contributed to the decline of minor league ball in many cities. People who could watch big leaguers on television just weren't very interested any more in the local bush leaguers.

Another sport that took on new life was boxing. Millions who had never before seen a match now tuned in every Wednesday and Friday to see top fights. Viewers at home watched Rocky Marciano become the new heavyweight champ and Sugar Ray Robinson win the middleweight crown.

Sport had no lack of great performers for all its ups and downs. Baseball admired Mickey Mantle, Joe DiMaggio's replacement in center field for the New York Yankees. Across the river from Yankee Stadium was the Polo Grounds, home of the New York Giants and another great center fielder, Willie Mays. And a subway ride away the great Brooklyn Dodgers teams led by Jackie Robinson, Roy Campanella and Duke Snider played at Ebbets Field. The Giants and Dodgers moved to San Francisco and Los Angeles in 1957, but during the '50s these three teams won 15 of a possible 20 major league pennants.

The new pro football interest centered around heroes like Johnny Unitas, quarterback of the Baltimore Colts, and the colorful Bobby Layne of Detroit. Hockey was dominated by Detroit's Gordie Howe and Montreal's Rocket Richard. In pro basketball, which was only beginning to attract a major following, two big men—George Mikan and Bill Russell—and little Bob Cousy drew the crowds.

But sports fans weren't just spectators—more and more of them were becoming participants. Bowling alleys went up by the thousands, and a pro circuit was established. Tennis attracted millions of new followers. And golf—a game favored by President Eisenhower himself—reached new peaks of popularity. In fact it was a golfer who provided the decade's first great moment in sport.

95

28

Ben Hogan Comes Back

When Ben Hogan was a ten-year-old boy he walked seven miles to caddy at a nearby course for 75 cents a round. He taught himself to play golf with a set of old clubs given him by a club member. The clubs were right-handed, and Ben was a lefty. So he learned a whole new skill to swing right-handed.

He became a pro golfer at 19 and was just beginning to succeed when World War II interrupted and he went into the Army. When he came out in 1945 the golfing world had forgotten him. He had to get back into shape and make up for lost time. Playing morning to night, hitting thousands of balls out of sand traps and out of the rough, he polished his game and hit the tournament trail.

He won five tournaments that year and was golf's top money-winner. In 1946 he won a really big one, the PGA Open, and earned the most money for the second straight year. By 1948 Ben Hogan was the most talked-about golfer in America. He

was an unsmiling, steely-eyed man who seemed to live only for golf. In that year he won the PGA again, the Western Open and then the U. S. Open, the most glittering crown of all.

The U. S. Open was held at the Riviera Country Club in Los Angeles. It was a murderous course, 7,021 yards long with some of the toughest sand traps anywhere. It was also very hilly, winding its way through Santa Monica Canyon. There was only one way to master it, as Ben Hogan well knew. A week before the tourney he began studying the course grimly. He got to know every bush, every blade of grass, every tree and hill, and each pebble of sand in the traps.

All that preparation paid off. By the third round of the tournament Hogan was putting all his shots together. His drives split the fairways; his putts dropped in. He shot a 207 for 54 holes, a new mark. On the final round he fired a blazing 69 for a 276 champion-

Ben Hogan sinks the winning putt in the 1948 PGA Tournament in St. Louis.

ship, five shots under the Open record. He was at the top of his game. He dominated the golfing world as nobody had done since Bobby Jones.

But then on a cold, wintry day the following year, Ben Hogan met disaster. On February 2, 1949, Hogan and his wife were driving from California to their home in Texas. Patches of fog swirled over the road. Suddenly, out of nowhere, a huge bus bore down on them. Neither driver could react in time, and there was a terrible head-on crash.

Valerie Hogan was barely scratched. But when Ben Hogan was pried from the wreckage, his body was smashed like the car. He was taken to a hospital in El Paso 100 miles away, and there doctors reported he had a double fracture of the pelvis, a broken collar bone, broken rib, broken ankle and severe internal injuries. Ben Hogan, the finest golfer in the world, came within a short putt of dying.

Two weeks later Hogan underwent delicate surgery to correct the internal complications. He was now out of danger, but his family and friends knew he would never play golf again. They read the physical signs correctly—no one with his injuries should even expect to walk again. But even his warmest supporters didn't reckon with Ben Hogan's toughness. He would get his smashed body into shape and play again—not only play, but win.

Almost immediately after the operation, Hogan began to plan his comeback. He squeezed a rubber ball to get strength back in his fingers. He did exercises for his patched-up stomach muscles. Soon he was jogging for miles. Friends watched in amazement as he went back onto a golf course just four months after his body had been smashed to pieces. Hogan was never a robust man— only 5-foot-8 and 135 pounds at his peak, he had been called the Bantam Rooster of golf. Could his small patched-up body ever withstand the rigors of pro championship golf now?

Frail but smiling, Hogan begins his painful comeback in a wheelchair in 1949.

Late in 1949 an official of the Los Angeles Open tournament received an entry from Ben Hogan. The official couldn't believe his eyes. The tournament was to be played in January 1950. How could a man so terribly injured plan to play golf after only eleven months? But when the tournament opened, Hogan was there. He rested on a chair between shots, and even casual observers could see that he was still wracked with pain. They predicted he would pick up his ball and call it quits after nine holes. But Ben Hogan shot a 73 the first day and three 69s to tie for first with Sam Snead. Although he lost to Snead in a playoff, Sam needed four birdies on the last nine to win.

No one doubted that Bantam Ben was back for good. In June, at Ardmore, Pennsylvania, he challenged a brilliant field in the U. S. Open. Fiercely, he attacked the course and his foes. He shot a first round of 72 but was eight strokes behind the leader. The following day Hogan shot 69. Now he was only two strokes back. The final 36 holes were to be played in one day. Could Hogan's body stand the strain? His legs and

Eleven months after his accident, Hogan tees off in the Los Angeles Open Tournament.

pelvic bones were one big, dull ache. After 18 holes he was in a four-way tie for second, one stroke behind the leaders. He came to the 36th hole needing a par to tie with George Fazio and Lloyd Mangrum. And he made a three-foot putt to force a three-way playoff the next day.

The playoff was no contest. Hogan led all the way and made a spectacular 50-foot birdie putt on the 17th. His 69 won the playoff by four strokes and gave him his second Open title—less than a year and a half after the accident. It was one of the most spectacular comebacks in all of sport.

Hogan went on to become the monarch of golf in his era. He won the Masters Tournament in 1951 and followed with a successful defense of his Open crown—his third. In 1953 he won the Masters, the U. S. Open and the British Open. An English sportswriter said it was a shame Hogan wasn't English—so that he could be knighted for his amazing accomplishments.

By 1960 Ben Hogan had won almost every major tournament of his time. But he would be best remembered for his spectacular play—against all odds—in 1950.

29

Giant Accomplishments

When an American League team moved into New York in 1903, it had to share a ball park with the New York Giants. Over the next 20 years, the Giants, led by John McGraw, were the most consistent team in baseball, featuring such stars as Christy Mathewson and Rube Marquard. The poor Highlanders—later renamed the Yankees—played second fiddle.

But by 1923 the tables had turned. The Yankees moved into their own new stadium and dominated the baseball news for the next 20 years. Now it was the Giants who were also-rans. By 1951 Giant fans were desperate as their team failed to win the National League pennant year after year.

The Giants' big competition in the National League came from the third New York team, the Brooklyn Dodgers. The Bums, as the Brooklyners were affectionately known, boasted one of the strongest teams in baseball. They won the pennant in 1947 and 1949. In 1950 they lost it to Philadelphia on the last day of the season. Now, in August of 1951, they were sailing along far ahead of the second-place Giants. On the

11th, they stretched their lead to 13 games.

Giant followers were about to give up when all of a sudden their team started winning. During the rest of August they won 16 games in a row. On September 1, they were only 5 games out of first place, and as September progressed they inched closer and closer to the top. On the last day of the season the Giants and Dodgers finished in a dead heat, each with 96 victories and 58 defeats. It was only the second time in major league history that two teams had tied for the pennant.

The National League winner—and World Series entry—would be determined in a three-game playoff. It would begin at the Dodgers' Ebbets Field and then move to the Polo Grounds for the last two games.

Led by their colorful manager Leo Durocher, the Giants were determined to make their miracle complete by beating the Dodgers. In the first game their determination paid off, and they took a 3–1 decision. The next day the Brooklyners gave Giant hopes a powerful blow with a 10–0 victory in front of a dispirited Giant crowd.

So the final game—destined to become one of the most famous in history—would decide everything. The Dodgers scored in the first as Jackie Robinson singled home a teammate. In the second inning the Giants should have scored but didn't. With a man on first, Giant third baseman Bobby Thomson got a solid hit to the outfield. He steamed around first and into second, only to find the other runner standing there, too. Before he could get back to first Thomson was tagged out. Giant fans shuddered. They knew their team couldn't afford to squander its chances.

New York finally tied the game at 1–1 in the seventh inning, but the Dodgers scored three times in the eighth. Two of the Dodger hits had bounced off Bobby Thomson at third base. Although he wasn't charged with an error on either play, Giant fans booed. Now things looked bleak for the miracle team. They failed to score in the bottom of

the eighth, and the Dodgers went out in the ninth. The Giants had just one more inning to get three runs for a tie and four for a win.

Alvin Dark, the first man up for the Giants, singled. Don Mueller also singled. Monte Irvin fouled out and slammed his bat down so hard that it broke. Then first baseman Whitey Lockman doubled, scoring Dark. Now it was 4–2 with one out and men on second and third. The Dodgers took out their starting pitcher Don Newcombe and brought in reliever Ralph Branca.

After Branca's warm-up pitches, Bobby Thomson, the goat of the second-inning mix-up, came to bat. Giant fans sat on the edges of their seats. If there was going to be a miracle, it would have to come soon. The first pitch was a called strike. Branca stared in. Thomson stared back grimly. Branca pumped, hoping to catch a corner with an off-speed fastball. Bobby Thomson swung, and the ball rocketed high and far.

Dodger left fielder Andy Pafko backed up to the wall, but as he followed the arc of the ball his shoulders sagged. It cleared the wall easily.

Halfway to first, Bobby Thomson saw the ball drop into the stands and heard the roar of the crowd. He ran and leaped and danced the rest of the way around the bases. When he touched the plate, the Giants had a 5–4 victory, thanks to the most dramatic homer in baseball history. The Giants nearly killed Thomson in their eagerness to congratulate him. Fans spilled out of the seats, whirling wildly in victory, and thousands of others rejoiced by their radios as the Giants' announcer mastered his excitement just long enough to tell what had happened. The Giants had come from 13½ games behind to win the pennant in the final inning of the last of three playoff games.

A poet had described the first gunfire by American patriots at Lexington in 1775 as "the shot heard 'round the world." But in 1951 the phrase was applied to the shot hit by Bobby Thomson.

The Homer: Bobby Thomson slams the ball, Dodger Carl Furillo watches it clear the wall . . .

The man in the on-deck circle when Thomson won the game was a young rookie named Willie Mays. Three years later Willie would produce a moment that rivaled Thomson's. The Dodgers won the pennant in 1952 and '53, but in 1954 the Giants won it again. Their World Series opponents were the Cleveland Indians, who had won 111 games in the American League, an all-time record.

The Indians' second baseman, Bobby Avila, was the American League batting champ, and center fielder Larry Doby led the league in homers. Cleveland's pitching staff included The Big Four of baseball: Bob Lemon (23–7), Early Wynn (23–11), Mike Garcia (19–8) and the great Bob Feller (13–3), who was in the twilight of his career.

The Giant roster hadn't changed much since 1951. But Willie Mays, who had been a rookie in '51, was now the best all-around player in baseball. That year he hit .345, blasted 41 homers, ran the bases with verve and played center field with incredible skill

—no easy feat at the Polo Grounds. Playing center field there was like playing in a cow pasture. The oddly shaped field measured 483 feet to straight-away center, and in some places there was a 50-foot wall. It was almost impossible for a hitter to get the ball out of the park in center—but it was equally difficult for most center fielders to cover all that ground.

The Indians scored in the first inning of the first game. First baseman Vic Wertz hit a towering triple with two men on to give Cleveland a 2–0 lead. The Giants tied the game in the third. Then in the eighth inning Cleveland put two men on base with only one out, and Wertz came to bat again.

Don Liddle, pitching for the Giants, pumped and threw. Wertz swung viciously, and the ball streaked out high and far to center field. In any other park it would have been a home run—and even at the Polo Grounds it should have gone for extra bases.

But at the crack of the bat, Willie Mays had turned and taken off as though he knew where the ball was going. There seemed no

. . . and Thomson's teammates mob him as he steps on home plate to win the 1951 pennant.

way for him to catch up with it—both Doby and Rosen would score and Wertz would have another triple.

Mays "traveled on wings of wind," as one writer wrote later. He never had a chance to

turn around. His back was still to the diamond as he reached up and out. It seemed that he never even looked around. Some instinct must have told him where the ball would be. It hit his glove—and stuck. In

The Catch: Willie Mays races from his position in center field (left) to catch Wertz's drive near the screen in right-center.

one motion he stopped, whirled and fired the ball to the infield to keep the runners from advancing. The next Indian batter went out to end the inning.

In the bottom of the tenth, pinch-hitter Dusty Rhodes slammed a home run with two on to win the game for the Giants. One of those on base was Willie Mays, who had walked and stolen second. And, of course, there would have been no tenth inning if Mays had not stolen those runs from the Indians.

The Indians never got over the shock of that first loss, and the Giants swept the Series in four straight games.

It would go down in history as the greatest catch ever made in a World Series, but in the locker room after the game, Willie Mays just grinned. "I thought I had it all the way," he said, and no one doubted him.

The Giants fell on hard times after 1954, and after the 1957 season they moved to San Francisco, deserting their rabid Polo Grounds fans. The Polo Grounds itself was torn down a few years later. But all these changes could never erase the great moments of the early '50s. Thomson's homer was still the "shot heard 'round the world," and Mays' outfield feat would always be known simply as "The Catch."

30

Speed Barrier at Indy

The Indianapolis 500 had come a long way since Ray Harroun won the first race in 1911, and so had auto racing. By the early 1950s racing had become a mania for millions of fans and participants. Stock car tracks were going up all over the South and Midwest, and a smaller group of enthusiasts was beginning to follow international Grand Prix racing. But the king of racing in the United States was still the Indianapolis Motor Speedway and its 500-mile race on Memorial Day.

Auto engineering had come a long way, too. In 1911 it had seemed incredible that cars could average 75 miles per hour over 500 miles. But 19 years later, in 1930, Billy Arnold broke the 100 mph barrier at Indy, averaging 100.448. It was another 19 years before Bill Holland pushed the mark above 120.

By 1952 the average was just under 130 mph. On the 2½-mile Indy track this meant that drivers had to accelerate to better than 150 mph on the straightaways and take the high-banked curves at breakneck speed. No one doubted that someday the 130 mph

barrier would be broken. The only question was who would do it.

On Race Day 1952 a young driver named Bill Vukovich almost did it. With only ten laps to go, he was leading by a half mile, and his powerful Fuel Injection Special was gobbling up the miles at a record rate. Then on the 191st lap a pivot pin cracked on his steering assembly. Vukovich screeched to a stop alongside a stone wall and raged silently to himself as Troy Ruttman passed him and won the race. Ruttman averaged 128.922 miles per hour.

"Wait till next year!" the frustrated Vukovich snarled as he slammed things around later in the garage.

In 1953 Vukovich qualified with the best time (138.39 mph) and started the race in the pole position—on the inside of the first line of cars. From the moment he crossed the starting line he was in command. It was a brutally hot day in Indianapolis, with temperatures soaring into the mid-90s. One driver actually died of heat exhaustion. Many others patted the tops of their helmets as they coasted into pit stops, the signal

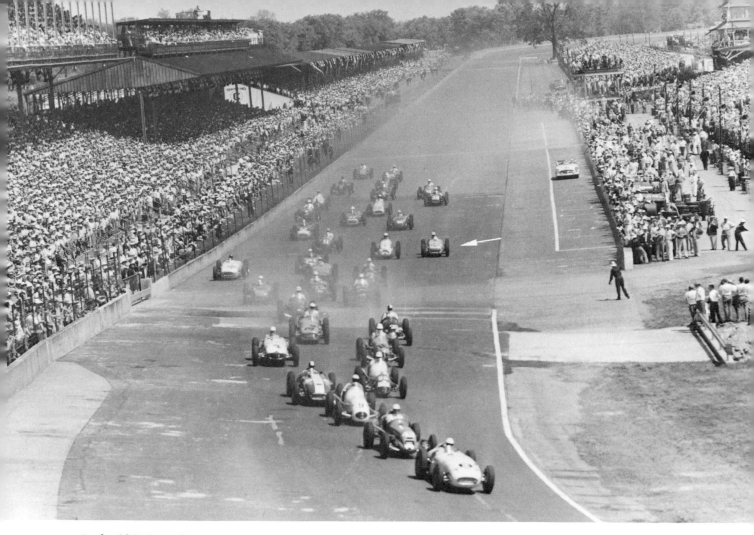

As the 1954 Indy 500 begins, Bill Vukovich is on the rail in 19th position (see arrow).

that they needed relief drivers. In fact, almost half the 23 starters who finished at least half the race that day, needed relief.

Twice during pit stops Vukovich poured cups of ice water down the back of his neck and roared right back onto the track. He drove the whole race himself, and he was never really challenged for the lead. At 250 miles he was four miles ahead of the second car, and at the finish he was eight miles ahead. He was pleased with his $89,000 prize money—but not with his average. He had averaged a fraction under 129 mph. The magic goal of 130 was still out of reach.

Throughout the next winter Vukovich became a physical fitness nut. He ran, swam and lifted weights to stay in top condition. Meanwhile, he and his mechanics nursed the powerful Fuel Injection Special with loving care. Every single part of the engine and suspension system was checked and re-

checked. The car was getting old, but Vukovich wanted just one more year out of it. Just 500 more miles plus a few miles of qualifying trials.

The powerful racing cars take a terrible beating at Indianapolis. A set of tires might not last more than 125 miles and must be changed at a pit stop. Steering mechanisms, carburetors and motors take terrific punishment from the constant vibration and the extreme temperatures that build up under the hood.

Before the race in 1954 reporters besieged Vukovich for interviews. They all wanted to know what he thought of his chances for winning his second Indy in a row. Consecutive wins were a rarity in the Indy 500: only two drivers had ever won two straight. Many fans believe the Indy race is a tougher task than anything in sports. In addition to a dependable car, a driver needs lightning reflexes, perfect eyesight and stamina to survive the heat, the noise and the pounding vibration. Most important, he needs courage because death is always lurking just around the next turn.

Bill Vukovich knew he already should have had two straight wins. The broken steering assembly pin in 1952 had cost him that honor. But as the 1954 race approached the confident racer acted like a man who had already won two and was counting on his third.

The day before the race he met a few of his rivals discussing the weather forecasts. "What're you guys talking about?" he asked straight-faced. "Trying to figure out who's going to finish second tomorrow?"

They laughed. Everyone knew that despite Bill's loving care his Injection Special had developed mechanical trouble. It had kept him out of the first series of time trials.

Dwarfed by the huge winner's cup, Vukovich accepts kisses from his wife and movie star Marie Wilson after his 1954 victory.

When his car was finally ready a week late, the first six rows in the starting line-up were already filled. His qualifying time was only good enough for 19th position.

The next day Bill Vukovich remained hemmed in position as the starter's flag sent the cars on their way, but in the first ten minutes he roared into seventh place. Jack McGrath, Troy Ruttman, Jimmy Bryan, Johnny Thomson, Jim Daywalt and Sam Hanks were out in front of him. Vukovich listened intently to his engine. It sounded sweet. He was ready to really turn it on.

The pace was blistering. Four of the leading seven had to stop for new tires around the 100-mile mark. At that rate they would have to stop for four tire changes. Vukovich determined to get as many miles as possible out of his tires—perhaps 150 miles. That way he would only have to stop three times. It was a risk, because if a tire blew out on the track he would be in big trouble. But if the tires held, he would pick up a crucial minute or two on the rest of the field.

At 150 miles he was in third place. On the next lap he took the lead but then finally made his first pit stop and fell back to fifth. But his strategy paid off. When the lead cars began making their second pit stops 30 laps later, Vukovich roared back into first place. By 300 miles he was a full lap ahead of his closest rival.

A growing murmur rose among the fans as his lap times were announced. Could he hold first place or would he—or his car— crack under the pressure? And what about the 130 mph mark?

Vukovich gambled again on his tires, making just one more pit stop. He lost the lead momentarily, but soon got it back. And most other drivers still had one more stop to make. As they dropped out for their final stops, Vukovich lengthened his lead and roared home a winner by more than a lap.

As he rolled to a stop in his pit, he was smothered by happy mechanics. Someone was screaming into his ear, but with all the noise he could hardly hear. It finally got through to him. He had broken through the 130 mph barrier with a new record of 130.840.

Later someone asked him how you win the Indy 500 with an average speed of more than 130 mph. Bill Vukovich smiled thinly as he replied, "You just keep your foot on the throttle and turn left."

He said nothing about the courage and incredible stamina it takes to drive 500 miles at that kind of pace. Finally, everything had gone right for Bill Vukovich, and he was at the top in the world of racing.

But the good fortune would not last. A year later, driving for an unprecedented third straight victory in the Indy 500, Vukovich was sideswiped by another car. His car careened into another and flew over the outer wall, end-over-end. It smashed into the ground nose-first, rolled several times, then burst into flames. When the rescue crews arrived, Bill Vukovich—the man who had dominated the Indy for four years and broken the 130 mph barrier—was dead.

31

A Perfect Game

Not all great moments in sport are provided by superstars. A case in point is the story of Don Larsen, a right-handed pitcher for the New York Yankees. No one had ever called him a great pitcher. In fact, many Yankee fans wondered why he was on the team at all. In 1954, with an admittedly poor Baltimore team, Larsen had the worst record in baseball: 3 wins and 21 losses.

In two seasons with the Yanks, he had compiled 9–2 and 11–5 records. But the Yankees were a great team. They didn't need to rely too heavily on Larsen. Manager Casey Stengel was practically a legend by 1956 when his team won its eighth pennant in ten years. With stars like Mickey Mantle and Whitey Ford and a cast of unremarkable but effective supporting actors, Casey could hardly lose.

Still, when he chose Don Larsen to pitch the fifth game of the 1956 World Series against the powerful Brooklyn Dodgers, some fans thought Stengel must be losing his touch. Larsen had already pitched—and lost—the third game. Now with the Series tied at two games apiece, why risk another loss by starting the erratic Larsen?

The Yankee batters would be facing Sal Maglie, who had won the first game. He was as shrewd and experienced as any pitcher in the majors. Now he would be opposing a young experimenter. Larsen had caused great curiosity by trying a no-windup, no-pump delivery. He just held the ball at his waist, then reared back and fired. The new style hadn't been particularly successful in the third game against the powerful Dodger batting order—Gil Hodges, Jackie Robinson, Duke Snider, Roy Campanella and others. And Yankee fans had little reason to believe that the fifth game would be any different.

In the first three innings both Maglie and Larsen retired every batter they faced. Then surprisingly, Maglie weakened. With two out in the fourth inning, Mickey Mantle hit a home run to give Larsen and the Yanks a one-run lead. The Yankees scored another run in the sixth, but by that time, attention was beginning to turn to Don Larsen.

After six innings the Dodgers still hadn't gotten a man to first base! Larsen had allowed no hits or walks, and the Dodgers had gone down in order. In the seventh he faced the top of the Dodger order—and put them down again, one-two-three. The crowd was

Above, pitcher Don Larsen fires the ball at a Dodger hitter in the 1956 World Series. At right, the scoreboard tells the story before Larsen's last pitch.

hushed when the Dodgers came up in the top of the eighth. Larsen pitched to Jackie Robinson, Gil Hodges and Sandy Amoros and sent them all back to the dugout.

Could this be? A journeyman pitcher was threatening to pitch a no-hit game, perhaps a perfect game, in the World Series. Only one other man had come close to a Series no-hitter. Floyd Bevens, another little-known pitcher, had come within one out of perfection in 1947. He too was pitching for the Yankees, and in the ninth inning he lost not only the no-hitter but the game—to the Dodgers—when Cookie Lavagetto doubled with two men on base. Yankee fans watching Don Larsen that day must have been remembering Bevens.

By the top of the ninth the pressure was intense. Broadcasters tried to keep their voices level. The official scorer wiped his brow—what if the no-hitter should depend on a close call between a hit and an error?

First up for the Dodgers was Carl Furillo, a dangerous batter in the clutch. He swung viciously at the first pitch and fouled it back. He swung at each of the next three and fouled them back. The suspense had silenced the crowd. Furillo swung again at Larsen's fifth pitch—but this time he sent a high fly ball to Hank Bauer in right field. One out.

Roy Campanella, the Dodger catcher and one of the most powerful sluggers in the league, was up next. He hit a grounder to second and was out at first. Two away.

The next batter was Dale Mitchell, pinch-hitting for pitcher Sal Maglie. He took the first pitch outside for ball one. He took the next pitch for a called strike. Still using his no-windup delivery, Larsen worked swiftly. Mitchell swung hard at his next pitch, and missed. Strike two.

The vast crowd seemed to inhale at once and hold its breath as Larsen came in with the next delivery. Mitchell fouled it off. The crowd groaned. Larsen threw again. This time Mitchell watched it go by. Umpire Babe Pinelli flung up his right arm. "Steee-rike" he shouted, and the crowd went wild. Yankee catcher Yogi Berra ran to the mound and jumped into Larsen's arms. The erratic pitcher had pitched a perfect game in the World Series!

The Yanks went on to win the Series in seven games. But the talk continued to be about Larsen. Had he suddenly become a great pitcher? His record in future seasons would prove that he hadn't changed much at all. But on that one day—October 8, 1956—Larsen had been as great as a pitcher can be.

32

Unitas Against the Clock

By 1958, Sunday afternoons had been established in millions of households as pro football time. Television had brought week-by-week coverage of National Football League games, and the audience was growing every year. Then on December 28, 1958, pro football gained new popularity. The game that afternoon, the NFL championship match between the New York Giants and the Baltimore Colts, would be one of the most exciting in the history of football. It set the stage for an even greater expansion of pro football interest in the years to come.

The Giants were Eastern Division champs. They had a slick quarterback, Charley Conerly; fine runners in Frank Gifford and Alex Webster; a great receiver, Kyle Rote; and a strong defense anchored by Sam Huff, football's best linebacker. The Giants had a 9–3 record and were slight favorites to beat the Colts, who also had a 9–3 mark.

The Colts had a young quarterback who only three years ago had been playing semi-pro ball for six dollars a game. He had been cut by the Pittsburgh Steelers, but he had a burning desire to be a pro. When he phoned the Colts and asked for a chance, they figured it would cost them nothing to take a five-minute look. They liked what they saw and signed him with no bonus for a minimum contract.

His name was Johnny Unitas, and within three years he had proven himself. He was cool under pressure, was a master at reading defenses, and had great ball-handling ability and a fine passing arm.

Unitas got lots of help from Lenny Moore, a swift halfback, and Alan (The Horse) Ameche, the league's best fullback. Raymond Berry, the target for many Unitas passes, was the best receiver in football. And there wasn't an offensive lineman in the league better than big Jim Parker. On defense, Gino Marchetti and tackle Big Daddy Lipscomb were terrors.

The championship game began as a defensive battle. Both teams failed on long first-quarter drives. First Sam Huff roared through the Baltimore line to block a Colt field goal attempt. A few moments later the Giants stalled on the Colt 36. Pat Summerall's field goal attempt was good, and the Giants went ahead 3–0.

Baltimore got the first big break of the game in the second quarter, recovering a fumble on the Giant 20-yard-line. Running backs Ameche and Moore carried twice each, and the Colts scored a touchdown.

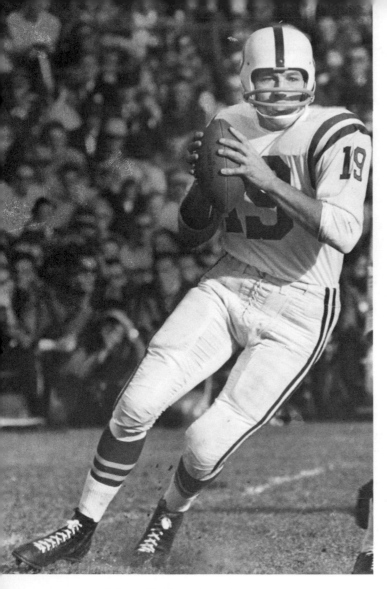

Johnny Unitas sets up to pass.

Leading 7–3, the Colts now had momentum. The Giants couldn't move the ball, and Unitas' running backs could. Johnny finally threw for a second touchdown. From the 15 he drilled the ball to Raymond Berry. At the half Baltimore had a 14–3 advantage.

Weeb Ewbank, then the Colts' coach, knew the Giants would come out blazing for the second half. He wanted another quick score to cool them off. A Colt drive went all the way to the Giant 3-yard-line, but against the tough Giant defense, it could go no farther. Now the Giants took heart. It was time to strike back.

Giant quarterback Charley Conerly hit Kyle Rote with a long pass. Rote caught the ball, then fumbled it, and Alex Webster scooped it up for the Giants and raced to the one-yard-line. One play later the Giants scored and it was 14–10.

Early in the fourth quarter two perfect pass plays brought the Giants another touchdown. Conerly pegged a 40-yarder off a fake reverse to end Bob Schnelker, moving the ball to the Baltimore 15. Then Conerly caught the Colt pass defenders napping as he threw to running back Frank Gifford for the score. Giants 17, Colts 14.

Then, with less than two minutes left, the Giants were faced with a fateful decision. They had the ball on their own 42, fourth down and one yard to go. They could keep the ball and try for the first down. If they succeeded, they could kill the clock and win the game. But if they failed, the Colts would take over in scoring range. So the Giants decided to punt. The Colts took over on their 14 with 1:56 left to play. Trailing by three points, they were in a desperate situation.

This was the kind of moment that would test Johnny Unitas' talent. When he saw the Giants protecting against the long bomb, he threw short. But his first two tries were incomplete. On third down, Unitas crossed up the New York defense by calling a pass to running back Lenny Moore. It was good for the first down. Then Johnny completed three straight passes to Berry for 62 yards. With less than ten seconds left, Unitas had the ball on the Giant 13. Steve Myhra came in to try the field goal from the 20. The ball was snapped, Myhra swung his leg, and the ball flew through the uprights.

Seconds later the gun cracked and the game was tied 17–17. Baseball ties are settled in extra innings and basketball games in overtimes, but usually in football, a tie is a tie. However, the National Football League had announced earlier that if this championship game ended in a tie, there would be a sudden-death overtime. The first team to score would win. Now the sudden-death overtime had come to pass—the first in pro history.

The Giants won the toss of the coin and

Alan Ameche carries the ball through a big hole in the Giant line to win for the Colts.

chose to receive. On their first drive they missed a first down by inches. They punted, and the Colts got possession on their own 20. A long 80 yards to go.

Unitas had already engineered one long pressure drive to tie the game. Now time was no problem, and it seemed he would stay on the ground to avoid risking an interception. L. G. Dupre got ten yards and a first down. After an incomplete pass, Dupre picked up three yards, and a pass to running back Alan Ameche brought a first down at the 40. Dupre carried again. Then Johnny was dropped for a big loss. It was third down. Unitas dropped back to pass, looking for Lenny Moore, but Moore was covered. Unitas spotted Ray Berry, but he was not out far enough to pick up the first down. Johnny coolly waved Berry out farther, then completed the pass.

The Unitas magic was moving the Colts again. They were at the Giant 42. Now Alan Ameche took the ball and stormed 21 yards through the surprised Giant defense. A pass to Berry brought a first down on the 9. Balti-

more was in easy field goal range, but Unitas was still moving the ball. The Giants expected him to stay on the ground now, but they did over-shift to cover Berry in case Unitas got reckless. So the cool quarterback decided to cross them up again. He stepped back into the pocket and lofted a short pass to tight end Jim Mutscheller on the other side. Mutscheller carried the ball to the one-yard-line.

On the next play Unitas slammed the ball into Alan Ameche's belly. The lines crashed together up front. Ameche hit a hole at tackle and burst over the goal line.

Final score: Colts 23, Giants 17. No one bothers with extra points in a sudden-death overtime. Besides, the field was swarming with thousands of Baltimore fans who had made the trip to Yankee Stadium to see their heroes. From that day on, Unitas was considered one of the top quarterbacks of all time. And after that dramatic game, millions of new fans devoted their Sunday afternoons to pro football, which soon became the most avidly followed spectator sport in America.

PART VII

1960-1969

The 1960s were an emotion-packed time—filled with hope and idealism, darkened by sorrow and fear. As the decade opened, an energetic young President named John F. Kennedy was elected. In his inauguration speech he proclaimed that Americans should "ask not what your country can do for you—ask what you can do for your country." Thousands of young people took his words to heart. They joined the Peace Corps, going abroad to help in underdeveloped countries, and interest in government increased by leaps and bounds.

Hawaii became the nation's 50th state (Alaska had been admitted in 1959). President Kennedy proclaimed the goal of putting a man on the moon, and in 1969 the amazing feat was accomplished. The movement toward equal rights for black people, which had begun in the 1950s, gathered momentum and resulted in rapid changes in laws and customs.

But the 1960s were also marked by tragedy. In 1963 an assassin's bullets cut down John F. Kennedy. Less than five years later assassins struck twice more. First Martin Luther King, Jr., a black leader in the civil rights movement, was killed in Memphis. A few months later Robert F. Kennedy, the late President's brother, was shot and killed as he campaigned for the Presidency. American cities—Los Angeles, Detroit, and others—erupted in bloody race riots, and the Vietnam war, the longest and most controversial in the nation's history, caused arguments that set brother against brother and son against father.

The pop singer of the decade was not any one person but a quartet of

A man on the moon . . . a president assassinated . . . and a crusade for equal rights.

shaggy-haired Britons called The Beatles who became superstars not only in America but all over the world. By now people had stopped dancing together, and something called "The Twist," started a whole new craze of free-style individualized dancing. Television remained the prime source of entertainment, and color sets began replacing black-and-white. Popular series such as "Gunsmoke," "Twilight Zone," "Route 66" and "Have Gun, Will Travel" ran each week for years.

For sports it was a decade of expansion. Major league baseball went from 16 to 24 teams. The American Football League, born in the 1950s, challenged the established NFL, and top college stars received hundreds of thousands of dollars as the leagues competed for their talents. The two leagues finally merged, bringing the number of top pro football teams to 26. Later in the '60s, the American Basketball Association was formed and competed for stars with the established National Basketball Association, which was expanding on its own. Hockey expanded, too, from the original six teams to fourteen, and for the first time pro teams were established on the West Coast. Televised sports events attracted ever larger audiences, and pro sports became a bigger business than anyone had ever dreamed possible.

In baseball Sandy Koufax of the Los Angeles Dodgers pitched no-hitters every season for four straight years, and his teammate Maury Wills broke Ty Cobb's single season base-stealing record with 104 thefts. The Yankees added to the excitement when *two* of the New Yorkers challenged Babe Ruth's single-season home run mark.

College football celebrated its 100th anniversary, and the Super Bowl was born. O. J. Simpson was undeniably the college star of the decade. Running backs Jimmy Brown and Gale Sayers and quarterbacks Bart Starr and Joe Namath were the biggest names in the pros.

In hockey, the great Gordie Howe was playing in his third decade; Bobby Hull broke all-time season scoring records, and a new superstar defenseman—Bobby Orr—emerged.

Pole vaulters with fiberglass poles were now flirting with 18-foot heights. U. S. domination of the Olympics was at an end, but America continued to provide many individual stars—swimmer Don Schollander, who won four gold medals in 1964; Bill Toomey, the 1968 decathlon winner; and many others. The winner of the Olympic light heavyweight boxing crown in 1960 was a handsome, polite youth from Louisville, Kentucky, named Cassius Clay —who would provide great moments and controversy in boxing in the years to come.

In tennis, Arthur Ashe became the first black to win the U. S. men's singles championships. The rising star in women's tennis was Billy Jean Moffitt who as Billy Jean King would one day bring women's tennis to renewed prominence. As the decade opened, golf was dominated by the remarkable Arnold Palmer. Wherever he played, Palmer was followed by huge galleries of fans who called themselves "Arnie's Army." But there was another player in the wings—a college student named Jack Nicklaus.

All in all, it was a prosperous age for sport—but even here there was room for conflict.

111

33

A Homer and an Asterisk

Since 1927 the most famous number in baseball had been 60—Babe Ruth's single-season home run record. It was a hard record to surpass, and many tradition-minded fans felt it never *should be* broken. In the 1930s Jimmy Foxx and Hank Greenberg had each hit 58, but since then no one had even come close.

Then in 1961 the New York Yankees boasted not one but two sluggers who seemed to have a shot at the record. The amazing Yanks were still going strong under the management of colorful Casey Stengel. Since 1947 they had won the pennant 11 times in 14 years, and in 1961 they were once more driving for a pennant. Another Yankee pennant race was hardly news, but the home run race had the fans in an uproar.

The two home run hitters on the Yankee squad were very different men. One was Mickey Mantle, who had been marked for stardom the day he replaced Joe DiMaggio in center field ten years earlier. The other was a quiet, sullen-seeming man named Roger Maris. Maris had always been a promising hitter, but never a great one—until 1961, that is.

Heading into September, Mantle had 48 homers and Maris had 51. Fans and sports-

The big bats for the Yankees: Mickey Mantle and Roger Maris.

writers began speculating on the home run record and the two modern challengers. Understandably, they favored Mantle—somehow it seemed fair that if anyone should do it, the new Yankee superstar should be the one. They had less to say about Maris—perhaps because he had less to say to them.

"Sluggers Ahead of Ruth's Record Pace" the sports pages exclaimed. But one had to go into September well ahead of the Babe. In that month alone he had hit 17 of his 60, an impossible act to follow.

There was another factor to consider. Ruth had hit his 60 homers in a 154-game season, but Mantle and Maris would have 162 games. What if one or another hit number 61 in one of the last eight games? How could you say they had broken the record? Joe Cronin, president of the American League, announced that a new record would count even if it took 162 games. Then the Commissioner of Baseball, Ford Frick, overruled Cronin and said that if 61 homers were not hit in 154 games, an asterisk (*) would go beside any record with a note explaining that the record had been set in a 162-game season.

By the middle of September one of the contenders dropped out of the race. Mickey Mantle went hitless in seven at-bats on September 14. After the game he told sportswriters, "Count me out." In 148 games he had only 53. Even to reach 60 he would need 7 homers in the 14 remaining contests.

Roger Maris said nothing. He had 56 homers for 148 games. Now all the attention centered on him—attention that his modest career had not prepared him for. By game 154 Maris had 59 homers—one less than Ruth had had in the same number of games. Roger couldn't win the record without the asterisk, but he had only to hit two more round-trippers in eight games to break the fabled 60. Maris still contended that it was the season, not the number of games that counted.

In game 158 Maris hit his 60th. Could he hit one more? The press and television announcers followed him day and night, asking questions, pleading for interviews. Maris even received hate mail from Ruth fans who didn't want to see the record broken.

Still, he had to try. Three games passed with no home runs. On the last day of the season the Yankees faced the Boston Red Sox. In the fourth inning Maris came up against pitcher Tracy Stallard. And for the 61st time in that '61 season he slammed the ball over the fence. He had broken baseball's most famous record, replacing "60" with "61*."

A few years later, Maris was traded to the St. Louis Cardinals. He helped the Cards win a pennant, but never again did he approach the magic 60. Fans remembered his 1961 feats but they never made him a superstar. Gradually he retreated from the spotlight, a reluctant record-breaker with nothing more to prove.

Maris follows through after hitting his 61st home run in the 1961 season.

34

Nicklaus Takes On the King

The husky, young blond golf pro self-consciously accepted a check at the end of the Los Angeles Open in January 1962. The check was for $33.33. That's thirty-three dollars and change. It was prize money for finishing in a tie for 50th place!

It was Jack Nicklaus' first appearance in a pro golf tourney, so his low finish wasn't really too surprising. But 22-year-old Jack Nicklaus was special, and for him 50th place was an embarrassment. He would have to be sharper than that if he was ever going to succeed in professional golf.

At age ten, Jackie Nicklaus had played his first rounds of golf at Scioto Country Club, near Columbus, Ohio. Within a year it became obvious that the youngster was something special, so his father sent him to the club pro, Jack Grout, for lessons. Grout watched the boy hit and whistled silently at his power. "You're going to be a hitter," he told Jackie. "So just let the horses go. Belt away with everything you've got. Your control will come later."

Two years later, at age 13, Jack Nicklaus shot a 69 at Scioto—a tough 7,095-yard course on which Bobby Jones had once won the U. S. Open. At 16 Nicklaus won the Ohio Open, beating the pros in their own event. And at 19, in 1959, he won the U. S. Amateur crown to become the youngest amateur champion ever.

In 1960 at the Cherry Hills Country Club near Denver, Nicklaus, still an amateur, came within two strokes of winning the U. S. Open. His 282 just fell short of the 280 posted by the King of Golf, Arnold Palmer. The two great golfers would meet again many times.

In 1961, as a junior at Ohio State University, Jack won the Big Ten and National

Jack Nicklaus follows the flight of the ball during the 1962 U.S. Open.

Collegiate crowns. Famed Buckeye football coach Woody Hayes, who had long known Nicklaus and admired his powerful swing, shook his head sadly. "What a waste of a great fullback," he said. "All that power and strength . . ."

The many faces of Nicklaus as he becomes the youngest Open champ in history.

That fall Nicklaus won the U. S. Amateur for a second time and decided to turn pro. A few months later, early in 1962, came his embarrassing 50th place finish in his first pro tournament. He was determined not to repeat that miserable performance.

By early June Jack Nicklaus had earned $25,000, more than any rookie in such a short time. The 50th-place finisher was improving every day. Now he was ready for the biggest test in golf—the U. S. Open, at Oakmont, near Pittsburgh.

The Oakmont course had more than 100 sand traps, and its lightning-fast greens were clipped to an eighth of an inch. Jack took notes on each tree, trap and road. He measured the distance from every hazard to the green. Like a general surveying a battlefield, he overlooked nothing.

Arnold Palmer didn't study the course this way. He didn't have to. Palmer had grown up in Latrobe, a few miles away, and had already played the course more than 200 times. But he would have been the tournament favorite in any case—he was the undisputed monarch of golf, having won more titles than any active player. His fans, calling themselves "Arnie's Army," always mobbed the courses when he played, cheering his every move and distracting his opponents.

As luck would have it, Palmer and Nicklaus were paired for the first two rounds. On the first day both were alternately brilliant and sour, with one-under-par birdies and one-over bogeys. Palmer finished with 71, Nicklaus with 72. Defending champ Gene Littler led the tournament with a 69.

On the second round Palmer was in top form. He shot several spectacular birdies and finished with a 68 to tie for the lead. Nicklaus managed to ignore Arnie's Army and concentrated on his game. He shot a fine 70, but now trailed Palmer by three strokes.

On the third round Palmer shot a 73, and Nicklaus inched closer with a 72. Even though they now had new playing partners, the real drama still focused on these two favorites. Nicklaus still had to pick up two strokes on the last round for a tie.

On the final round Jack Nicklaus played methodically, almost grimly. He birdied several early holes, then refused to yield to the pressure in the homestretch and finished with seven straight pars and a score of 69.

At one point, Palmer flubbed a shot for one of the few times in his brilliant career, and the ball trickled only ten feet. But he recovered and reached the 18th hole with a chance to win—if he could sink a twelve-foot birdie putt. Carefully he studied the green, then addressed the ball. He tapped it lightly, and the ball broke left of the hole. Nicklaus' 69 and Palmer's 71 left them in a tie. The next day a playoff would decide the title.

Arnie's Army was at its noisiest for the playoff. But Jack Nicklaus was at his iciest, and he used some psychology of his own. He deliberately slowed down his game, taking much more time than usual between shots. Palmer was plainly irritated at times, and his concentration suffered. He bogeyed three of the first eight holes while Nicklaus had one birdie, so Jack led by four strokes. But Palmer was a great clutch player. He mounted one of his famous "charges" and birdied the ninth, eleventh and twelfth. Now he was down by only a stroke.

Palmer couldn't keep it up, however, and Nicklaus could. Arnold needed three putts on the 13th, while Nicklaus kept booming those 290-yard drives, chipping crisply to the green and putting brilliantly. Nicklaus finished with six straight pars for a 71, while Palmer bogeyed the 18th and final hole to post a 74. At age 22 the Buckeye Belter, who looked more like a fullback than a golfer, was the U. S. Open champion.

In the next ten years Nicklaus would win more major tourneys than any golfer in history. His 1973 PGA title gave him a total of 14, one more than the 13 won by the immortal Bobby Jones. With years of golf still ahead of him, he had surpassed Palmer, Hogan, Jones and every other golfer. But his first great step came in that 1962 playoff when he challenged and beat the King.

35

The Sting of the Bee

A heavyweight championship fight was scheduled in Miami, Florida, on the afternoon of February 26, 1964. The day of the match, two things were clear. First, few people wanted to see it; fewer than 7,000 tickets had been sold in advance. It would be the smallest heavyweight title crowd in 40 years. And second, nobody thought the challenger belonged in the same ring with the champ. In fact, some even doubted that the challenger would show up.

The champion was Sonny Liston, and the challenger was Cassius Clay. It was reported that Cassius Clay, at the noon weigh-in, had been almost hysterical. He had trembled, blubbered strange things and acted like a man going to his doom.

And why shouldn't he?

Sonny Listen had won his title by knocking out champion Floyd Patterson in the first

As Sonny Liston is examined at the weigh-in, he is heckled by Cassius Clay (top).

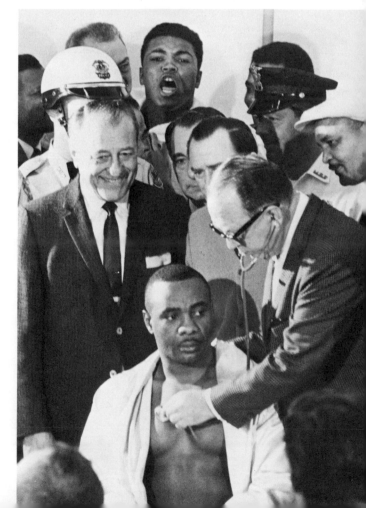

round. Ten months later in a rematch he had kayoed Patterson in the second. Altogether he had knocked out 25 of his 36 pro opponents. Sonny Liston was a sullen, cruel fighter who could half-scare his foes into defeat just by glowering at them across the ring. The rest of the job he did with his thundering fists.

Clay, the 22-year-old challenger, had won the Olympic gold medal in the light-heavyweight class in 1960 and turned pro shortly thereafter. He soon became famous for his endless bragging, his handsome face and the amateurish doggerel poetry he spouted before every fight. As he progressed through the heavyweight ranks he began to compose a little rhyme before each bout, telling the round in which he would knock out his foe. He fought few headline heavyweights but, strangely enough, he did knock out many opponents in the round he predicted. He was a fast, classy boxer. As he said, "I float like a butterfly and sting like a bee!"

The public reaction was mixed and confused. Some thought Clay's antics entertaining, but many others called him obnoxious and foolish. But almost everyone agreed that Sonny Liston would destroy him in two rounds at most. Only three of the 46 boxing writers covering the fight thought Clay even had a chance. On the day of the match, the odds were 8–1 against him.

By fight-time there were only about 8,200 in the Miami arena. Clay made a theatrical entrance, dancing down the aisle and doing a little jig in the ring. Liston entered a few minutes later, a hood partially covering his sullen face. The hooded robe made him look like an executioner who only wanted to get the job done as soon as possible.

With the opening bell Liston stalked out flat-footed. He missed with three menacing swings and then landed a solid right. The crowd roared. What they had expected seemed about to happen.

But then Liston couldn't catch up with Clay for another solid punch. Clay gracefully dodged the champ's jabs, retreating in a circle around the ring. Something strange was going on. Then late in the round Clay hit Liston's face with a hard left and sent a quick, savage barrage of blows to the champ's head. The crowd was amazed.

In the next round Liston furiously tried to maul the challenger into a corner or against the ropes, but Clay kept dancing out of trouble. Then several of Clay's fast left jabs sneaked through Liston's defense. He followed with a hard right, and a surprised look came over Liston's face. The champ began to bleed from a gash on his left cheekbone.

Liston plunged after Clay like a bull the next two rounds. Once he caught Clay with a long left, but he was already too tired to take advantage of it. Ringside experts were amazed at Clay's speed. By comparison, Liston seemed to be working in slow motion.

In the fourth round the crowd murmured strangely as Clay seemed to taunt Liston with insults and paw his own face with his glove. The truth was that something had gotten into Clay's eyes. He was in pain and was having trouble seeing.

By the end of the fourth Clay was in agony. He begged his trainer, Angelo Dundee, to cut off his gloves so he could get to his smarting eyes. Dundee assured him the problem would go away and ordered him to continue, but to stay away from Liston until his vision cleared. Liston could see that Clay was in trouble and tried desperately to get to him in the fifth round. But the champ couldn't catch him. Soon Clay's vision cleared and he began flicking his jab in Liston's face, often following with a hard right. By the middle of the sixth round it was clear that Clay's dazzling speed and fast hands would cut Liston down before the 15th round.

At the end of the sixth Sonny Liston went slowly to his corner, but he didn't sit down. His trainer, his second and a ringside doctor milled around him while the crowd won-

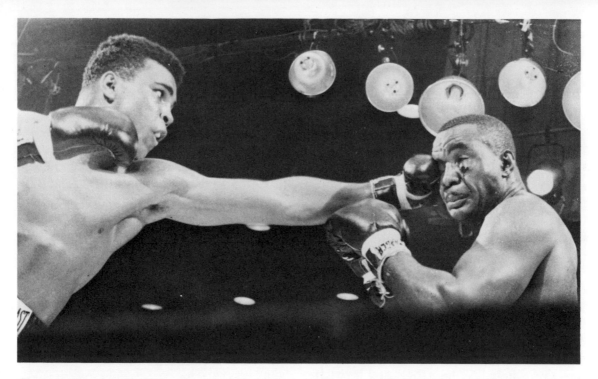

Clay punishes Liston in the third round (above) and goes wild after winning the fight.

dered what was going on. When he finally sat down, Cassius Clay danced to the center of the ring and triumphantly waved his hands high in the air. Then he was being hugged by his trainer, Dundee, and his assistant, Drew Brown.

There was bedlam in the ring as the announcer tried to tell the crowd that Liston

could not come out for the seventh round because his shoulder was injured. It would be listed as a technical knockout.

Fans and writers at ringside were incredulous. The handsome young braggart was the new heavyweight champion.

Twenty minutes later in his dressing room Cassius Clay faced a crowd of writers and screamed at them. "Whatcha gonna say, now? You said Liston would put me away in one round! Eat your words! Eat your words!" He kept raving about how beautiful he was and how he was the world's "mostest" and greatest champion ever, and the writers could do nothing but stand there and take it.

Cassius Clay later became a member of the Black Muslim sect and changed his name to Muhammad Ali. He soon proved he was one of the great heavyweight champions, defeating Liston again, Floyd Patterson and a host of lesser challengers. Then he refused to be drafted into the Army during the Vietnam war, claiming that he was a minister in the Black Muslim religion. His claim was later upheld by the courts, but during nearly five years of legal argument, state and national boxing associations refused him permission to fight. Since he was not able to defend his title, he lost it by default. But even fans who disliked Clay could grant that his first fight against Sonny Liston was one of the dramatic moments in boxing history.

36

Sayers Runs for Six

George Halas, owner-coach of the Chicago Bears, had seen more great moments in football than any man alive. He had been an original incorporator of the National Football League. Such stars as Red Grange, Bronko Nagurski, Sid Luckman and Johnny Lujack had played for his Bears. Then in 1965 another of his players turned in an epic performance.

His name was Gale Sayers, a rookie running back. Right away Halas knew Sayers would be a future star, but he let him start out the season slowly. Gale watched most of the first three games from the bench, although he played enough to score two touchdowns in the third one.

In the fourth game Halas finally started Sayers, and the rookie got another touchdown. By the fifth game the team, the fans and the press sensed what Halas already knew—that Gale was far more than just another rookie.

His history had been spectacular. He had been a prep star at Omaha Central High School, and in three years at the University of Kansas he had rushed for 2,675 yards (6.5 yards per carry). Sayers had speed (9.7 for the 100), exceptional power, balance and cutting and faking skills. He also had an uncanny ability to see running room where none seemed to exist.

In his fifth game for the Bears he put it all together in a wild 45–37 win over the Minnesota Vikings. He scored four touchdowns, and it was clear that Gale Sayers had arrived.

By the time the Bears met the San Francisco Forty-Niners in the last game of the season, Sayers had led Chicago to eight straight victories. By now he had tallied 16 touchdowns, just four short of the NFL season record of 20.

The turf at Wrigley Field, Chicago, was soggy that December Sunday. At game time it began to drizzle. The going would be slippery for the runners, and the Forty-Niner defense was pleased. A slippery field might make it easier to stop Gale Sayers. After the first play from scrimmage, however, the Forty-Niners could see that the muddy sur-

The Bears' great rookie, Gale Sayers, in 1965.

face wasn't going to make much difference to Sayers. He slashed 17 yards for a first down.

Two minutes later, after an exchange of punts, Sayers took a screen pass from quarterback Rudy Bukich, got two good blocks and wove his way through four more Forty-Niners for an 80-yard touchdown.

With about five minutes remaining in the second quarter, the Bears had a 13–7 lead and possession at the San Francisco 21. Sayers took a hand-off and angled toward left end. Suddenly, he spotted a hole in the line. With lightning reflexes he cut, went into high gear and ripped through, going all the way to the goal line. Four minutes later, with time in the half running out, the Bears had the ball on the San Francisco 7. Sayers again took a hand-off from Bukich, swept wide and cut back in for the score—his third in the first half. The Bears had the lead, and Sayers had a chance at the season touchdown

record. He had 19, and the old mark was 20.

Early in the third quarter Bukich again pitched out to Sayers on the San Francisco 48. This time Gale flashed around end and flew past a defensive halfback on the way to his fourth touchdown.

The game was becoming a rout. With three minutes left in the third quarter, the Bears had driven to the Forty-Niner one-yard-line. But it was fourth down. The defense expected Sayers to carry the ball wide. He carried the ball, all right, but exploded straight into the middle. He was hit at the goal line, but his momentum carried him up and over two defenders and into the end zone. He had scored five touchdowns in the game and broken the season record with 21. Now he was just one touchdown away from tying the one-game record of six set 35 years earlier by Ernie Nevers of the Chicago Cardinals.

Then Halas took his star out. This tremendous talent was too valuable to risk long after the game was won. But 46,000 fans screamed for more. Finally Halas gave in. Sayers returned in the fourth quarter as a safetyman on a Forty-Niner punt. It was murky and wet as the ball descended to Sayers on his own 15-yard-line. At least five tacklers came charging down on him, but he fielded the ball cleanly and streaked straight upfield. He burst between the first two men and cut left, streaking past two others. Only one man now had a chance to catch him, but Sayers faked past him with a change of pace and was on his way to another score. It was an 85-yard touchdown run, his sixth of the day, and tied Nevers' mark for a single game.

Sayers left the game again with the Bears ahead 61–20. Halas put him back in for the final play of the game on a Forty-Niner kick-off. It would be Gale's one shot at a seventh touchdown. He took the ball on the 19, sped upfield and made his cut to get into the clear. But this time he slipped on his cut and was brought down. One more good step and Gale Sayers might have scored again.

Sayers flies into the end zone for his fifth touchdown of the game.

But the crowd had seen the greatest ground-gaining performance ever put on by a pro halfback. Not only did he score six touchdowns, he gained 336 yards in total offense, a staggering one-game total.

Sadly, Gale Sayers had few chances to repeat the magic of that game. The next season he suffered the first of a series of knee injuries. He had several operations and returned valiantly to the line-up, contributing all he could. But the injuries robbed him of the extra split-second of speed and the unbelievable maneuverability he had shown as a rookie. As with many athletes, his greatest moment came early. But it would be remembered with awe by all who had seen it.

37

The Fastest Mile

For the first half of the century, the most famous miler in track history was Paavo Nurmi, "The Flying Finn." When he set a new world mark in 1923, a Finnish newspaper ran a full-page picture of the stopwatch with the hands frozen at 4 minutes, 10.4 seconds.

The world's best milers kept chipping away at that mark until it came down around 4:05. Then fans began talking of the impossible 4-minute mile. In 1945 Sweden's Gunder Haegg ran the distance in 4:01.4, and the race toward a record under 4 minutes was on.

Progress was slow, however. Finally, on May 8, 1954, Englishman Roger Bannister broke the barrier with 3:59.4. He had cut eleven seconds off Nurmi's old world record and two seconds off Haegg's 1945 time. It had taken nine years to chop off those last two seconds! In the following years a number of other runners broke 4 minutes, and

gradually the record was reduced—half a second here, another fraction there.

According to track experts the mile was an event for mature men. While sprints might be won by schoolboys, most of the world-class distance runners were in their late 20s and early 30s. They had trained for years, developing strength, stamina and ability to withstand the searing pain of running past exhaustion.

But then in 1964 a Kansas schoolboy appeared at the Compton relays in California to compete against a strong international field of milers. He didn't win the race, but he finished in 3:59.0, becoming the youngest runner ever to break four minutes.

His name was Jim Ryun, and at the age of 17 he showed unlimited potential. That summer he qualified for the U. S. Olympic team, but in Tokyo he caught a bad cold and finished ninth of ten finalists in the 1,500-meter "metric mile." In the spring of 1965, however, Ryun showed what he could do. In his second appearance at the Compton relays he finished third to Peter Snell and Jim Grelle, but he crossed the finish in 3:56.0. Three weeks later he beat the same two runners and lowered his best time to 3:55.3. When he was in top shape, the young Ryun *expected* to run in less than four minutes.

That fall he entered the University of

Roger Bannister breaks the 4-minute mile in 1954 (above). In 1964 Jim Ryun (below) became the first teenager to crash the barrier.

Kansas and began preparing for the next track season. From the moment the 1966 meets began, it was clear that Ryun might change the record book. In the Compton relays he won the mile in 3:53.7, only a tenth of a second slower than the world record held by Michel Jazy of France.

Then came a big surprise. Six days later, in the U. S. Track and Field Federation Championships at Terre Haute, Indiana, Jim entered the 880-yard run (the half-mile). In the preliminaries he ran it in 1:51.0, good enough to qualify, but far from Peter Snell's world record of 1:45.1. But two hours later in the finals, everything fell into place for Ryun. The keepers of the stopwatches couldn't believe their eyes as he broke the tape. Jim Ryun had set a new world record of 1:44.9 for the half-mile!

Five weeks later Jim was ready to add a second world record. He entered an All-Star meet in Berkeley, California, with the intention of running the fastest mile ever. The field included no one who could really challenge him, but Jim went out to race against the clock. He ran extraordinarily fast first laps of 57.7 and 57.8, for a halfway time of 1:55.5. The track fans in the crowd knew that the record was in danger, and they began to cheer. His third lap was timed at 59.8. Now how much would he have left? Ryun said later that he tried and tried to accelerate on that last lap and couldn't. But at least he wasn't slowing down. He ran it in 58 seconds flat, for a new world record of 3:51.3. The new time was a full two seconds faster than the old record.

It would seem that no runner could surpass Ryun's 1966 performance. But in 1967 he still had more to offer. On the evening of June 23, Ryun led a strong field of milers in the National AAU meet at Bakersfield, California. Seven of the eight entrants, including the young high school star Marty Liquori, were capable of breaking four minutes. By this time, Ryun himself had broken it in twelve different races.

It seemed that Ryun might use a field like this to help push himself to a new record time. It was his usual tactic to stay off the pace in the first three laps. Then he could pick the right psychological moment and run away from the field in the stretch with a mighty finishing kick.

But soon after the gun sounded for the start of the mile that night in Bakersfield, the 10,000 fans were startled to see Ryun take the lead after the first 200 yards or so. As he loped past the starting line after the first lap, his time for the first quarter-mile was announced as 59.5. It was a good time but not a great one. The knowledgeable fans knew that it was far off Ryun's world record pace the year before.

After half a mile the young Kansan extended his lead to more than ten yards. Dedicated fans checked their own stopwatches, while others waited for a report from the official timer. The split for the second quarter was 59.5 seconds. The first half mile had taken 1:59.0.

Fans exchanged glances. Ryun would need to pick up the pace in the third quarter and give a blazing kick down the homestretch to even approach record time.

Jim Grelle and Tom Van Ruden, Ryun's strongest competitors, tried to close the gap on the third quarter, but Ryun was picking up the pace. His long legs kicked out just a tiny bit faster as he maintained his lead. As he came around the final turn on the third leg everyone knew it would be his fastest split yet. It was. He did the third quarter in 58.6. His accumulated time was 2:57.8. Now even a slow 60-second last lap would break four minutes, but Ryun's sights were set higher.

When the gun signaled the final lap, Ryun opened up as though beginning a 440-sprint. He had run the whole race in first place, and there would be no catching him now. With no opponents to push him, Ryun would have to push himself. Going into the final curve where he usually started his kick to catch a

After the race, Ryun catches his breath while timers check their watches: 3:51.1.

front-runner, Ryun now launched a kick on his own behalf.

His lungs must have been burning, his muscles on the verge of collapse. But distance runners learn to ignore pain. "I was feeling fine," he recalled later. "Everything was dropping into place just right—my stride, my strength, my kick—everything."

Fans were amazed as Ryun sprinted into the last 100 yards. He was running faster than any miler had ever run on the last lap. Some of the fans with stop-watches were so excited they forgot to click them as Ryun broke the tape. The official timer announced the time of 3:51.1, a new world record, two-tenths of a second faster than Ryun's old record. He had run the last quarter in an incredible 53.5.

Never satisfied, some sportswriters began suggesting a sub-3:50 mile. But such a feat would not happen soon. Ryun's time proved itself remarkable as year after year left it unmatched. At 22, Jim Ryun had already approached the limits of human excellence.

38

Basketball's Big Men

As the 1960s progressed, basketball—both college and professional—grew rapidly in popularity. The college game had been shaken by gambling scandals in the 1950s, and the National Basketball Association was still fighting off its image as a small-town league. But by 1965 television was picking up important games, tickets were increasingly hard to get, and basketball players were becoming the highest-paid athletes in America.

Much of the credit for basketball's new popularity belonged to three big men: Wilt Chamberlain, Bill Russell and Lew Alcindor (later known as Kareem Abdul-Jabbar). By most standards all basketball players are big, but these three were giants, both in size and in their influence on the game.

A few months before Jim Ryun ran his record mile, Wilt Chamberlain and the Philadelphia 76ers had set a new record for excellence in pro basketball. In the 1966–67 season the 76ers won 68 and lost only 13. With stars like Hal Greer, Billy Cunningham and Chet Walker it was clearly a good team. But Wilt made it a great team. Standing well over 7-feet tall and weighing 280 pounds, he could intimidate any player in the league on offense or defense. During the regular season he averaged 24.1 points per game. More amazing, he also averaged 24.1 rebounds and nearly 8 assists per game.

In his seven years in the league Chamberlain had nearly taken ownership of the NBA recordbook. One season he *averaged* 50.4 points per game. In one game, against the New York Knicks in 1962, he scored an even 100. His rebounding and defensive feats were the talk of basketball. There was only one problem. Wilt's teams never won the championship, and Wilt himself suffered from comparison to the league's other big guy, Bill Russell of the Boston Celtics. Russell couldn't score like Wilt and he wasn't as big (6-foot-9), but he was the greatest defensive player basketball had ever seen. More important, his Celtics had won eight NBA championships in nine years.

Going into the '67 playoffs, Wilt and the 76ers were determined to stop Boston for a change. During the season, Wilt had changed his style to complement the team. His scoring average was the lowest in his career, but unlike other seasons, he was now playing at both ends of the court, taking on a bigger share of the defensive burden.

Philadelphia rolled over Cincinnati in the first round of the playoffs and then roared into Boston to test the great Celtics in the semi-finals. After years of playing second fiddle to Russell, Wilt finally drove his rival into the ground. The 76ers took the best-of-seven series in only five games. In one contest Chamberlain picked off 41 rebounds, still a playoff record. In the final game Philadelphia buried the Celtics 140–116.

Now Chamberlain not only owned the record books, he had a championship as well. Nevertheless, Wilt was by no means the sport's only attraction. Soon he would share the spotlight with another giant.

In the fall of 1967 attention turned to college ball. The defending national champion was UCLA, led by a man even taller than Wilt Chamberlain. He was a senior named Lew Alcindor. In his two varsity seasons with UCLA Alcindor had led them to two straight NCAA titles. In fact, the team had lost only one game since he started and was

Giant Wilt Chamberlain takes a rebound from Bill Russell in the 1967 NBA playoffs.

now embarked on a long winning streak. As the '67–68 season moved into high gear, the streak stretched past 40.

Experts believed that there was only one team in America that might topple UCLA. The University of Houston had a great center named Elvin Hayes. The two teams had met in the finals of the 1967 NCAA tournament, and UCLA had won. But they were scheduled to meet again in the regular '67–68 season, and the game was advertised as the college contest of the year.

It was played before a roaring crowd in Houston. Several days earlier, Alcindor's eyeball had been scratched during a game. His vision was still a bit blurred, but he refused to use that as an excuse. Cheered on by their rabid fans, Houston played a great game and just managed to edge out the Bruins 71–69. Their winning streak was ended at 47, but the UCLA team was not about to fall apart. They didn't lose another game all season and won each game through the early rounds of the NCAA post-season tournament. Then in the semi-finals they were paired against Houston once again.

Now the tables were turned. The NCAA tourney was being played at UCLA's own Pauley Pavilion, so the home crowd would be with the Bruins. Actually, the Bruins didn't really need a cheering section. They

UCLA's Lew Alcindor hooks over Elvin Hayes of Houston in the 1968 NCAA semi-finals.

were already fired up enough. The players lost so rarely that they heartily resented the few teams that beat them. So now they were looking to teach Houston a lesson.

To say that UCLA beat Houston would be an understatement. When the final buzzer sounded the score was 101–69. Alcindor scored 19 points and got 18 rebounds, but the statistics that told the most were Elvin Hayes's. The Big E, playing against more than 7-feet of defensive toughness, scored a lowly ten points and pulled down only five rebounds. Seldom in the annals of college basketball had one highly touted team so outclassed another. The next night the Bruins beat Purdue in the finals to win their third straight national championship, but it was almost anticlimactic. As Kareem Abdul-Jabbar, Alcindor would go on to win championships in the NBA, too, but his performance against Houston would be remembered as one of his greatest moments.

There was plenty of action on the pro circuit, too. At the beginning of the 1968–69 season, things had changed somewhat. In the year since Wilt Chamberlain had won his championship, Chamberlain himself had been traded to the Los Angeles Lakers, making that team the greatest in basketball history, according to some experts. Out of five starters, three Lakers were true superstars: Wilt, Jerry West and Elgin Baylor. They were like an All-Star team that plays together all year.

The other surprise was the decline of the Boston Celtics. The perennial champions stumbled so badly during the '68–69 season that they finished fourth in their division, barely qualifying for the playoffs. Bill Russell was now the coach of the team as well as its star center. Most of the Celtic regulars were over 30, and several of them seemed to be slowing down. As the long season progressed, the Celts seemed to be losing the energy and the drive that had sparked their play for so many seasons. Russell was nearly 35, and he was finding the additional burden of coaching especially difficult. When the playoffs began, fans were already regretting that this great player could not end his career on a winning note.

But Boston had a few surprises for their critics. In the first round of the playoffs they beat a determined Philadelphia team (without Wilt) in five games. Then in the semifinals they beat a tough New York Knick team in six. Most of the games were close and hard-fought, and the Celtics were counted out several times. But whenever the game was at stake, Russell became his old self, holding the Celtics together, scoring the crucial basket and harrying the enemy shooters.

It wasn't easy, but Boston finally qualified to meet the "all-star" Los Angeles Lakers in the playoff finals. One more time Russell and Wilt Chamberlain would square off against each other. Wilt had often complained that the reason Russell won so often was that Russell played on better teams. This time, however, the shoe was on the other foot. Wilt would lead the sparkling Lakers against a tired and aging Celtic team, a fourth-place finisher. Although the Celtics were sentimental favorites, experts gave the Lakers a wide advantage.

Playing the first two games at home, the Lakers won a squeaker in the first, 120–118, then took the second as well. The experts were looking good. Jerry West scored 53 and 41 points, and Chamberlain, playing the new "team" style he had used a year earlier in Philadelphia, was outmuscling Russell.

Still, the Celtics wouldn't give up. In the third and fourth games, at Boston, they got even by scores of 111–105 and 89–88. Then Los Angeles won game five to take an advantage of three games to two. Now the Celts had their backs to the wall. They needed two straight victories to win the championship, the first in Boston and the second back in Los Angeles. In his last appearance before the home crowd in Boston,

An aging Bill Russell works his defensive magic on Wilt in the 1969 NBA playoffs.

Russell once again demonstrated his genius as the Celts held the high-scoring Lakers to only 90 points and won 99–90.

But winning the last one away from home would be more difficult. Boston went out to a big lead early in the game, but the Lakers, led by Jerry West's scoring and Wilt's rebounding, whittled it down through the last two quarters. With three minutes left to play, Boston was ahead by just one point, 103–102. How could the tired old men—Russell in particular—hold on any longer? No one was ever sure how they did it, but they did, leading 108–106 at the buzzer.

Bill Russell announced his retirement as a player soon after that triumph. Chamberlain continued to play, and within a few years he led a team even better than the 1966–67 76ers. And that summer Lou Alcindor was drafted by the Milwaukee Bucks, making that expansion team an almost immediate threat for the NBA championship. Between the three of them, they had already helped make basketball one of America's top spectator sports.

39

Broadway Joe's Super Bowl

In 1960 the fashionable hairstyle for men was the crewcut—hair cropped short enough to stand up by itself. But as the decade progressed, longer and longer hair came into style. Parents were horrified when their teenagers began to worship the Beatles. The English rock group let their hair grow down past their collars—and even over their ears.

For a while it seemed that athletes would resist the trend and stick to the traditional short hair. But then along came Joe Namath.

Namath first came into prominence in 1964 as a hot-shot passer for the University of Alabama. In 1965 he led the Crimson Tide to the Orange Bowl and was considered the finest college passer in the country. His hair was still fairly short, but he already had a reputation as a maverick off the field. Alabama coach Bear Bryant threatened him often for his off-hours misbehavior and even suspended him once.

No one could fault Joe's actions on the field, however. In his senior year he became the object of a fierce battle between two football circuits—the established National Football League and the upstart American Football League. The new league had been in operation for five seasons but was still struggling to stay afloat. The owner of the AFL team in New York recognized the promise of greatness in Namath, and the Jets finally signed him for a huge bonus. Most fans hardly knew that the New York Jets existed, and many found it hard to believe that Namath would go to the bush AFL rather than the NFL.

Namath was worth every penny the Jets paid. His personality brought lots of new attention to the league. And his football savvy and throwing arm became the nucleus of a championship Jet team. The Jets struggled through 1966 and 1967, even with "Broadway Joe," as the long-haired passer was sometimes known. But in 1968 he led them to the AFL championship.

The team was coached by Weeb Ewbank, the man who had assembled the famous 1958 Baltimore Colts. With a fine defensive squad, good running backs in Matt Snell and Emerson Boozer, and great pass receivers in George Sauer and Don Maynard, the Jets were strong, at least for the AFL. But whether they liked him or not, most people agreed that Joe Namath made the big difference.

Now that they had the AFL title, the Jets would play in the Super Bowl against the NFL champion Baltimore Colts. Two years earlier the NFL had reluctantly agreed to a post-season championship game. In the first two Super Bowls the NFL's Green Bay Packers had had no trouble proving their superiority over the AFL champs.

There was no way the Jets could be favored in Super Bowl III. It was the difference between the leagues, said the experts. The Jets might be colorful, but they would be lucky to avoid a sound beating at the hands of the Colts. By the week of the game the Colts were 17-point favorites.

But one man disagreed—Joe Namath. From the time the Jets arrived in Miami for the game, he spoke of a Jet victory with confidence. A few nights before the game Namath and teammate Jim Hudson were having dinner in a restaurant when Colt place-kicker Lou Michaels came in. Namath looked up and said with a grin, "Michaels, we're going to blast you out of the park next week."

Michaels predicted none too humorously that Joe would be spending most of the game flat on his back. The needling got rougher, and the two almost came to blows. Word got around. Joe repeated his prediction. "There's no way we'll lose," he told reporters.

Joe Willie's confidence must have been catching. Early in the first quarter the Colts recovered a Jet fumble on the Jets' 12 but were unable to score. The Jet defense stopped Baltimore's running attack cold and then intercepted a Colt pass in the end zone.

Taking the ball on the 20, Namath mixed running plays featuring Snell and Boozer with passes to George Sauer and Bill Mathis to take the Jets all the way to a first down on the Colt 9-yard-line. The Orange Bowl crowd couldn't believe that the 17-point underdogs were knocking on the Colts' goal line.

Snell slammed through the middle of the line for four. Then it was Snell again, deceiving the defense by going around end for the touchdown.

The Colts tried to put on their own drive after the Jet score, but they couldn't get past the Jet 41. Baltimore's field goal attempt was wide, and Joe and his Jets left the field with a 7–0 halftime lead. The Colts would be playing for blood as well as victory in the second half.

But the Colts stumbled again when Tom Matte fumbled early in the third quarter and the Jets recovered. A moment later Jim Turner kicked a Jet field goal from the Colt 32, and the score was 10–0. The heavily favored Colts were still frantically trying to get untracked—with little success.

Joe Namath that day was truly the super quarterback. Time and again he read the Colt defense and called plays at the line of scrimmage to take advantage of its weaknesses. When the Colts dropped back to protect against the pass, Joe sent Snell blasting through their line. When they were expecting the run, he passed.

Then late in the third quarter Joe finally got dumped by a Colt rush and jammed a

Controversial Joe Namath calls signals and Matt Snell carries in the 1969 Super Bowl.

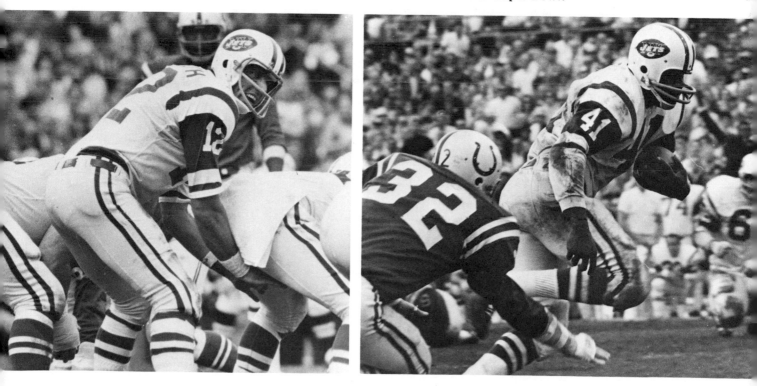

thumb. He had to leave the game and was replaced by back-up quarterback Babe Parilli. Maybe now the Colts could finally get a rally going. But before they even got the ball, the Jets had driven to the 30 and Jim Turner had booted another field goal. The Jets led 13–0.

The next time the Jets got the ball, Namath tested his thumb. It still hurt, but this was a moment to forget about pain. He ran onto the field and began another drive for the Jets. Again he kept the Colts off-balance, and he reached the Colt 9-yard-line before being stopped on a fourth-down situation. In came Jim Turner who kicked a field goal to make it 16–0.

The Colts had to get something going soon or it would be too late. Already they needed at least three scores to win. In came the aging veteran, John Unitas, hero of so many Baltimore success stories. He had worked miracles before. Maybe he could work another. On his first drive he took the Colts to the Jet 25 but failed to score. On his second try he was superb, completing four passes and finally putting points on the board for the Colts. It was now 16–7, and the Colts lined up for an on-side kick, hoping to get possession of the ball on the play. The bounding ball bounced off a Jet and the Colts came up with it. Now Unitas had another chance. But the Jet defense smelled victory. The front four rushed Unitas on the next three passes, and he threw three straight incompletions. On fourth down Unitas dropped back again. There was another furious rush by the Jets. Unitas fired to Jimmy Orr, one of his favorite receivers, but Jet linebacker Larry Grantham leaped up in front of Orr and batted the ball away. The Jets took possession, and the Colt threat was ended.

When the gun went off minutes later, the New York Jets had done the impossible. An American Football League team had defied the odds and the experts. They had gotten superb quarterbacking and passing from Joe

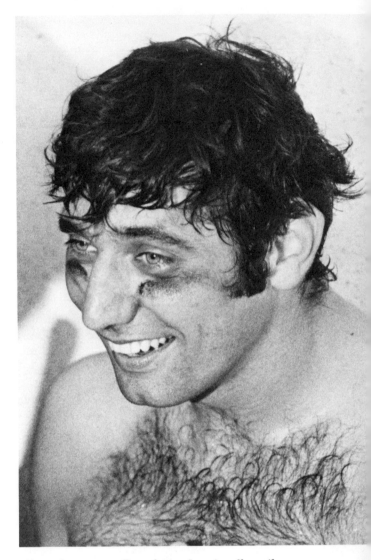

After the game, Broadway Joe is all smiles.

Namath, who completed 17 of 28 passes for 206 yards. And they had gotten a great game from fullback Matt Snell whose 121 yards in 30 carries had ripped the Colt line apart to set up the passing game.

From then on there was no doubting the AFL teams. Soon after the Jet victory the two competing leagues agreed to merge. Within a few years AFL and NFL teams were competing every Sunday. Living up to the boasts of Joe Namath, the AFL held its own and was finally recognized as truly equal.

40

The Amazing Mets

The Stadium-mates of the Super Bowl champion New York Jets were a rag-tag baseball team—the New York Mets. When the major leagues had first expanded in 1962, a new National League team came to New York to replace the Giants and the Dodgers, who had both moved to California.

Of course, no one could replace those two great teams—but the Mets didn't even come close. In fact, they were the most inept team in major league history—a collection of cast-offs and misfits from other clubs, and a few youngsters of fuzzy and uncertain future. Their manager, former Yankee boss Casey Stengel, told the fans, "Come and see my amazin' Mets," and the name stuck. Casey spoke the truth. The Mets were amazingly bad. The fans came to see the new team by the thousands even though the Mets lost 120 games and won only 42 in their first season, the worst mark in big league history.

The Mets lost 100 or more games each of their first four seasons, finishing tenth of ten teams each year. In their fifth year they climbed to ninth place, then dropped back to the cellar the next season. In 1968 they finished ninth again, but things were looking up.

By this time their manager was Gil Hodges, the popular former first baseman of the Brooklyn Dodgers who had worked wonders managing the Washington Senators. Hodges told reporters before the 1969 season began that he expected his Mets to win at least 85 games that year. He had begun to see signs of hope toward the latter part of 1968. Someone reminded Hodges that if the Mets won 85 games, they would be in the first division. With a straight face, Hodges said, yes, he knew that. Everyone else laughed.

The Met team was not overloaded with well-known players. They had a tremendously promising young pitcher named Tom Seaver. Bud Harrelson was one of the best fielding shortstops in the game, but not a strong hitter. Outfielders Cleon Jones and Tommy Agee were promising hitters, but no one claimed they would ever rival Willie Mays. Nevertheless, die-hard Met fans, who had followed the team through seven dismal seasons, were soon delighted to see their team playing .500 ball.

On August 15, the Mets were in third place in the National League's Eastern Division. This was the first year the majors were split into divisions. Cynical fans pointed out

One of the Mets' 1969 heroes: Tommy Agee.

that even with the worst record in baseball, the Mets would have to improve in 1969—after all, they could finish no lower than sixth because there were only six teams in their division. The Chicago Cubs, solid favorites to win the division race, were 9½ games ahead of the Mets. Still, even a third-place finish would be a huge improvement for the New Yorkers. Perhaps in three or four seasons they might really challenge for a pennant.

The Mets continued to play well. On September 4, they returned to New York after a road trip only five games behind the Cubs. A few optimistic fans suggested that the Amazings could still pass the Cubs. And in the next few weeks a curious fever took hold of New York City as the Cubs began to slip. On September 8 they came to New York for two games, only 2½ games ahead. The Mets chopped them down 3–2 as rookie pitcher Jerry Koosman struck out 13, then picked up a 7–1 win on Tom Seaver's five-hitter. Was this a dream? In September the Mets were only a half game from the division lead!

On the night of September 10, the Mets beat Montreal in a twi-night double-header and the Cubs lost to the Phillies. Now the Mets were in first place, and New Yorkers were talking of little else. There were still 21 games left, and doubters waited for the Mets to fold. But they never did. During September they won 23 and lost 7, winning 10 straight at one point.

Then on the night of September 24, history was made at Shea Stadium. Donn Clendenon hit two homers and pitcher Gary Gentry gave up only four hits as the Mets beat the Cards 6–0 to clinch first place in the Eastern Division. The Amazing Mets had amazed everyone—they had suddenly become amazingly *good*.

Now the Mets would face the powerful champs of the National League West, the Atlanta Braves, in their very first championship playoffs. With sluggers Hank Aaron and Orlando Cepeda as well as a good pitching staff, the Braves were strong favorites to win the best-three-of-five series. The Mets, a no-name club by comparison, would learn that superior talent wins in the end—so said the experts.

But the Mets' talent prevailed once more. They blasted home nine runs in the first game to answer the critics who called them light hitters. The final score was 9–5. The next day they did it again, outslugging the Braves 11–6 with home runs by Tommy Agee, Ken Boswell and Cleon Jones. The Amazings were averaging ten runs per game! The shell-shocked Braves gave up, losing the third game and the playoff 7–4. Now the Mets had two miracles.

But could the upstarts defeat the Baltimore Orioles in the World Series? Three miracles in one season for a team that had

Pitcher Tom Seaver is lifted in the air after beating the Braves to win the pennant.

After the Mets win the World Series, exultant players and fans jump for joy.

never before finished better than ninth in their league? No! said the experts. The Oriole batting order was the strongest in baseball, featuring Frank Robinson, Boog Powell and Brooks Robinson. And their pitchers—20-game winners Mike Cuellar, Dave McNally and Jim Palmer—were just as impressive.

When Tom Seaver pitched the first game against Cuellar in Baltimore, it seemed the Met magic had finally run out. Seaver was driven out of the game, Cuellar pitched well, and the Orioles won 4–1.

In the second game the Mets had a 1–1 tie in the top of the ninth. Second-stringer Ed Charles got on second base, and then little Al Weis singled him home for the winning run. Now the Series was even.

The next three games would be played in New York's Shea Stadium. For thousands of the faithful, this was the payoff. Met banners flew from windows all over town as game three began. The Stadium, filled to the rafters, seemed to shudder as thousands of fans roared, "Go-o-o Mets!" Young Gary Gentry pitched, and Agee and Ed Kranepool provided homers. The powerful Oriole batters were hand-cuffed, and the Mets won 5–0.

In the fourth game Seaver came back. He had been disappointing in the first game, but in front of the home fans he dueled with Baltimore ace Mike Cuellar into the tenth

inning. The score was tied 1–1. The Mets put a man on second base in the tenth. Then pinch-hitter J. C. Martin bunted. Pitcher Pete Richert's throw went past the first baseman after hitting Martin, and the lead runner scored all the way from second. Mets' game, 2–1.

The fifth game would be the last in New York, and Met fans wanted it to be the last in the Series, too. Rookie pitching sensation Jerry Koosman gave up only five hits to the hapless Orioles. Donn Clendenon and Al Weis hit Met homers, and the one-time clowns were the world champions.

The joy in New York knew no bounds. Horns blew, confetti poured down from windows and strangers greeted each other on the streets with a salute to the Mets. The Amazings had kept their name but reversed their fortunes.

In Baltimore, the sentiment was altogether different. That January the New York Jets had upset the Colts in the Super Bowl. Now the New York Mets had upset the Orioles in the World Series. The poor Baltimore fans hardly dreamed that still another defeat was on the way. But at the end of the 1969–70 basketball season the New York Knicks upset a strong Baltimore Bullet team in the playoffs and went on to win the championship. Three winners in a row for New York—and, against all odds, three losers for Baltimore.

PART VIII

1970-PRESENT

With the election of Richard Nixon in 1968 it seemed that the turmoil of the 1960s would soon be over. In his inaugural address the President promised to bring the country together again after the violence and disagreements of the '60s.

As the new decade opened, the Vietnam war was still in progress, although the number of American fighting men was declining. But American bombing was increasing. Soon the President would order the invasion of Cambodia and the mining of the major North Vietnamese harbor at Haiphong. Anti-war demonstrations broke out on college campuses across the land. In some cases, the National Guard was called out, and at Kent State University in Ohio four students were killed by a volley of fire from Guardsmen.

In 1972 the President was reelected by a great landslide of votes, and the negotiations to end the war finally seemed to be succeeding. Then, just as it seemed that the nation might return to tranquility, the greatest political scandal in a century began to break. In June 1972 six men paid by the President's reelection committee were caught breaking into the offices of the opposition party.

At first little attention was given to this incident. But by mid-1974 the government had been shaken by a flurry of resignations, indictments and convictions of high officials. To make matters worse, inflation and shortages of petroleum products sent prices up and up, causing widespread dissatisfaction. As the United States approached its 200th anniversary in 1976, its political and economic future was uncertain.

134

Tragedy and death at Kent State . . . a celebration by mustachioed ballplayers . . . and the nomination of a new vice president.

Sports continued to create memorable moments nonetheless. Continuing the trend toward long-haired athletes, the world Champion Oakland A's sported a record number of exotic mustaches and beards. In 1972–73 the Miami Dolphins won 17 straight games, including the Super Bowl. And they repeated as champs the following year. O. J. Simpson set a new season rushing record in 1973, gaining more than 2,000 yards.

Basketball and hockey competed for attention during the winter. Expansion had brought them new fans in many different parts of the country. In college basketball the UCLA Bruins won every national championship from the days of Lew Alcindor through 1973. In January 1974 they ended sports' greatest winning streak at 88 games.

Jack Nicklaus continued to dominate golf. In 1973 he won his 14th major tournament, surpassing the record set by Bobby Jones. Tennis was rapidly gaining public favor, as both men's and women's matches reached national television. The fight of women to gain equal billing and prizes, led by champion Billie Jean King, brought about one of the strangest sports spectacles of the century.

Boxing, which had hobbled through the late 1960s after Muhammad Ali's departure, regained some of its old glitter. Ali came back to meet the new champion, Joe Frazier, in an event billed as the "Fight of the Century."

But the first great moment of the decade was provided by the brightest star of the fastest-rising game in sports. His name was Bobby Orr and his game was hockey.

41

A Stanley Cup for Bobby

Hockey fans saw what was happening through the 1969–70 season but weren't prepared to believe it. Defensemen don't do a lot of scoring in the NHL. They manage to knock in a goal once in a while, but if they do it a dozen times a season it is rare. What they are supposed to do is knock the enemy forwards loose from the puck and help defend their own goal.

Then why was 23-year-old Bobby Orr scoring all those goals for the Boston Bruins from his defense position? By the end of the season the answer was in—although nearly everyone had already been sure of it for a couple of years. Bobby Orr, then in his fourth big-league season, was revolutionizing the game. He was doing things defensemen weren't supposed to do, picking up dozens of goals and scores of assists. Bobby had speed, slick stickhandling, an uncanny sense of position on ice, and bruising toughness. He was the greatest defenseman hockey fans had ever seen. But he was more—many were saying already that he was the greatest all-around player ever.

During the regular season Bobby had led the Boston Bruins to a first-place finish in the NHL's East Division. Only three years earlier, the Bruins had been a hapless cellar-dwelling club—and they had not won a Stanley Cup since 1941.

Leading the way to the regular season triumph, Bobby had scored 33 goals and made 87 assists for 120 scoring points, breaking his own record for a defenseman set the previous year. He was the first defenseman ever to lead the league in scoring points and was named best defenseman and most valuable player. But for the fans, this was merely an appetizer for the feast to come in Stanley Cup action.

Hockey's biggest star and most revolutionary influence: Bobby Orr of the Boston Bruins.

The Bruins had whipped the New York Rangers and the Chicago Black Hawks in the first two rounds, blasting the strong Hawks out in four straight games. Now they faced the St. Louis Blues for the Cup.

The Blues, an expansion team, were only in their third year in the NHL. They were something of a Cinderella Club. But Bobby Orr's stick was a magic wand in reverse; for the Blues, midnight would come with a rush.

The Bruins clobbered the Blues in St. Louis in the first two games. Orr flashed all over the ice for goals and assists. As the series came to Boston for games three and four, Bruin fans were thinking about a rare four-game sweep. And sure enough, in game three Orr was shooting, checking, making deft assists, capturing stray pucks in a 4–1 victory.

Now the Bruins were just a game away from the coveted cup. But the Blues were going to give it their best shot. Among their assets was veteran goalie Glenn Hall, one of the greatest in the game. The Blues even went ahead, 2–1, in the second period, but the Bruins tied it up. Then back came the Blues after the intermission, scoring in the opening moments to go ahead again.

But the Bruins were too close to victory to give up. Captain Johnny Bucyk scored on an assist by John McKenzie, and the game went into sudden-death overtime, tied 3–3.

The Bruins were one goal from winning their first Stanley Cup in a generation, and Bobby Orr was the man who would get it for them.

The countdown to that moment had been spectacular. Bobby had started playing hockey at the age of four. By the time he was twelve he was famed as Canada's most promising juvenile league player. At 5-foot-2 and 110 pounds he was already being scouted by the pros who marveled at the way he slashed his way across the ice with the drive and coolness of a 20-year-old.

The Boston Bruins won the battle for his services when he was 14, getting his parents to sign him to a Junior "A" card. Critics said he was ready for the NHL at 16, but league rules forbade the Bruins from bringing him up until he was 18. The Bruins' general manager had already said he wouldn't trade Bobby Orr at 16 even for the entire Toronto Maple Leaf team.

When Bobby turned 18, the NHL found out why. The league's best forwards discovered he could hit like a football lineman, he could carry the puck as though it were attached to his stick, and he could accelerate like a dragster.

In his first season, 1966–67, he fired 13 goals into the nets and had 28 assists for 41 points—a brilliant beginning that won him the Calder Trophy as rookie-of-the-year. In his second season he won the James Norris Trophy as the best defenseman. In 1968–69 —after two knee operations—he zoomed to 21 goals, 43 assists and 64 points and again won the Norris Trophy, setting a new point-scoring record for defensemen.

In 1969–70 Bobby Orr owned the hockey world outright with his all-around play, almost doubling his points total and leading the Bruins to a first-place tie. Then came the playoffs, and the final overtime period against the Blues.

The Bruins' Derek Sanderson snared the face-off and flicked the puck to the Blues' end of the rink. Bobby Orr daringly pursued it instead of doing the normal thing and dropping back on defense. In the race for the rubber, the Blues got there first and tried to clear it to their offensive zone.

Bobby Orr had come too far down the ice to give up on the situation now. Boston fans roared as he flashed his stick and stole the puck from the Blues' Larry Keenan. Almost with the same motion he backhanded it along the boards to Sanderson behind the Blues' net. What followed was classic.

After stealing the puck and passing it to Sanderson, Orr was now flashing from right to left in front of the goal. Now he was sliding his stick over the ice for Sanderson's return pass. It came, and with a snap of his wrist Orr swept the puck past goalie Glenn

As Orr's Cup-winning shot goes in, he is tripped from behind (above). A moment later, his teammates gather around him to begin celebrating their victory.

Hall and into the net just as a Blues defenseman caught Bobby's foot with his stick.

Orr cartwheeled through the air and landed sprawling on the ice. His vision of the net was obscured for an instant as he flew through the air, but the roar of the crowd told him everything he needed to know. He had scored. The Stanley Cup belonged to the Bruins for the first time in 29 years.

42

The Fight of the Century

In 1967 Muhammad Ali was excluded from boxing under a cloud of suspicion and dislike. Thousands believed that he was an unpatriotic draft-dodger when he refused to report for induction to the Army during the war in Vietnam. Early in the year he had successfully defended his heavyweight title against Zora Folley. Shortly afterward he was indicted for refusing to report and for the next several years, the case was in the courts—and Ali was banned from the ring.

During that time, however, public opinion about Vietnam began to change. By 1970 some boxing authorities were beginning to wonder why Ali should not be allowed to fight. His supporters claimed that he was being unjustly treated. Although he had been accused of a crime, his case was still in the courts, and there was reason to think he might not be convicted.

Finally, the city of Atlanta made the first move to allow Ali to fight again. Many were still bitterly opposed to his views and actions, but there was little doubt that heavyweight boxing had been less exciting since his absence. In October 1970 Ali stepped into the ring in Atlanta to fight heavyweight contender Jerry Quarry.

The big question was whether Ali's three-year layoff from the ring had hurt him. Apparently it hadn't because he scored a three-round technical knockout over Quarry. Now the stage was being set for the most lucrative heavyweight championship match of all time. Muhammad Ali would fight the new reigning champion, Joe Frazier, and settle once and for all the arguments about his skill as a fighter.

Joe Frazier? Well, he was a sort of temporary champion. Like Ali, Frazier had been an Olympic champ (1964). Then he

Talkative as ever, Muhammad Ali (formerly known as Cassius Clay) appears on TV.

too had turned pro and battled his way to heavyweight title contention. After 19 straight victories he had been matched with Buster Mathis for the New York State version of the world title, which had just been taken away from Ali. On March 4, 1968, Frazier kayoed Mathis in eleven rounds and was recognized as the champion in six states.

The World Boxing Association held a separate elimination and settled on two

Joe Frazier stings Ali with a hard left hook (above). At right, in the 15th round, Ali is knocked down for the first time in his pro career.

finalists: Jimmy Ellis and Jerry Quarry. Ellis beat Quarry for the WBA crown, then met Frazier for the undisputed championship.

The bout took place in New York on February 16, 1970. Frazier pounded Ellis all over the ring, and when Ellis failed to answer the bell for the fifth round, Joe Frazier was named the world heavyweight king.

But many fans kept thinking: "What about Ali?" Joe Frazier would never be the undisputed champ until he beat the outlawed favorite.

A Frazier-Ali match edged closer to reality in 1971 when the Supreme Court announced it would review Ali's draft case. Public antagonism toward the ex-champ had begun to melt, and even before a decision was handed down, promoters decided to take a chance. They signed the fighters to a contract that would pay them a record $2.5

million each. The fight would draw 3,000,-000 fans into movie theaters around the world for live closed-circuit television. In addition, a capacity crowd of 20,000 would jam Madison Square Garden in New York after paying the fanciest prices ever for a prize fight. It would be the biggest fight of all time.

When both men went into training, Ali became the blustering loud-mouth of old. But it was still not clear what the long layoff would do to his speed and timing. Experts who had watched the Quarry fight warned that Ali was not his old self.

On March 8, 1971, Frazier and Ali climbed into the ring for the most bally-hooed fight since Jack Dempsey's return match with Gene Tunney. Scalpers got $500 for ringside tickets. Police surrounded the Garden with barricades and vans. Black fans turned the evening into a fashion show, as

TV cameras recorded their arrival in the most ornate clothes ever seen at a fight.

Even the fighters were the most elegantly-styled in memory. Ali appeared in red velvet trunks and Frazier in green and gold brocade. But once the fight started, the fashion show was forgotten—the two champions staged a brawl worthy of their appearance.

As usual, Ali had made a pre-fight prediction: "Frazier will fall in six," he'd boasted.

In the early rounds the confident Ali put on a show, winking at ringsiders and chattering insults at Frazier. He seemed to be in complete control. But then in the fourth round Frazier bloodied Ali's nose. Ali suddenly became more serious, but he still kept up some of his clowning.

Although many fans weren't aware of it, both men had been connecting solidly. The sixth round came and went—Ali's prediction was wrong. As the fight continued, both of Frazier's eyes seemed swollen and Ali's face was puffed. Both fighters were bleeding from the nose.

Ali caught Frazier with a good flurry in the tenth but couldn't move in for the kill. In the eleventh round Frazier scored with a vicious left hook, and another left to the body slammed Ali onto the ropes. No longer floating like a butterfly, Ali barely got through the round on rubbery legs.

By the 14th round both fighters were in bad shape, but neither was willing to fall. Frazier was bleeding freely from his mouth and a cut over an eye, but ringside observers still thought he had a slight advantage.

In the 15th Ali came off his stool with a rush, sensing the need for a big finish. But Frazier refused to back-pedal. He uncorked a terrific left that sent Ali tumbling backwards onto the canvas for a solid, dramatic knockdown. It was the first time in his pro career that the self-proclaimed "greatest and most beautiful" had ever gone down. He got up, and Frazier connected with another left. Each was trying to put the other away in those last desperate seconds.

Then the final bell. A couple of moments later the referee announced the verdict: Frazier by a decision. The fight had been close, and Ali later claimed he was robbed. But most people who saw the fight agreed with the judges. Joe Frazier had done it. He'd won the now-undisputed heavyweight title.

However, both men had taken a terrible pounding. Frazier went into a Philadelphia hospital and stayed ten days. Even Ali, who usually emerged from his fights unmarked, took many days to heal and recover. Almost immediately, there were demands for a re-match. And finally, in January of 1974, the two fighters met again. But some strange things had happened in the meantime. Joe Frazier had lost his heavyweight title to young George Foreman, and Ali had been beaten by an unknown challenger named Ken Norton.

Ali got revenge on Frazier, beating him soundly in a twelve-round decision. But the magic wasn't there. The two fighters, older and slower, had to give way to Foreman, the new young champ.

43

Mark's Seven Medals

In late August 1972 in Munich, Germany, Mark Spitz was poised at the most dramatic moment of the world's greatest swimming career. By his own estimate, as the Olympic Games opened, he had swum the equivalent of once around the world. Ahead, less than a mile remained for him to prove whether he was the greatest of all time—or another bust as he had been four years earlier at the Olympics in Mexico City . . .

By the time Mark Spitz was 17 he was one of the world's best swimmers in the free-style and butterfly stroke. He had set or tied five American records and had broken five world marks. Just out of high school, Spitz had gone to the Mexico City Olympics in 1968 vowing to win five gold medals—three individual and two in the relays. He was a handsome and promising young man, and he was supremely confident—if not boastful. His prediction of five golds was quoted in newspapers and magazines all over the world.

He turned out to be a flop. Although he won golds in each of the relays, Spitz failed to win any of his three individual events. He took a silver in the 100-meter butterfly, a bronze in the 100-meter free-style and was dead last in the 200-meter butterfly.

All kinds of reasons were given for his failure: He had a cold; Mexico City's high altitude bothered him; he had been troubled by conflicts with his more modest team-mates.

Now, four years later in Munich, he was a vastly different Mark Spitz. He was stronger, and handsomer. Many swimmers shave their heads before important races to eliminate every bit of "drag" in the water. Spitz not only had a modishly long head of hair, he sported a mustache! More important, he was wiser—and quieter. Although he was the center of attention on the U. S. team, this time he made no predictions.

But the experts and the newspapers said Mark Spitz had a good crack at *seven* golds. The great Paavo Nurmi and Jesse Owens had won four each. So had American swimmer Don Schollander. And an Italian fencer named Nedo Nadi had once won five.

But seven golds? If the world's best swimmers didn't foil Spitz, the pressure would. As fate would have it, before Spitz finished his seven events, the games were interrupted by terrible and tragic events. Arab terrorists kidnapped eleven Israeli Olympians, and all eleven eventually died. Since Spitz was Jewish, there was even fear for his personal safety. That was the kind of pressure few athletes ever had to face.

But now, on August 28, Mark Spitz crouched on his starting platform at the Olympic pool for his first event. He shook his fingers and arms one final time. The bell sounded, and Mark Spitz hit the water for the 200-meter butterfly. He won by six feet in 2:00.7, for a new world record. Mark Spitz had his first gold.

After his three failures in Mexico, it was his first individual Olympic crown. But that was only the beginning.

Just 30 minutes later, Dave Edgar, the lead-off man for the U. S. 400-meter free-style relay, hit the water for the first leg. John Murphy took the second leg, Jerry Heidenreich the third. As Heidenreich touched the wall, Mark Spitz launched himself for the anchor leg. He churned home well ahead of the second-place Russian anchorman. The Yanks had turned in a world record time of 3:26.42, and Spitz had his second gold.

The finals of the 200-meter free-style were held the next day. Steve Genter, an-

Mark Spitz swims the butterfly on his way to his first gold medal at the 1972 Olympics.

other American, was primed for an upset, but Spitz came from behind to nip him at the finish for another world record, 1:52.78. Gold number three and world record number three for Mark Spitz.

The 100-yard butterfly came next. Canada's Bruce Robertson was considered Mark's toughest challenger, but the American super-swimmer beat Robertson by more than a body length in 54:27 for his fourth world record and his fourth gold.

Forty minutes later, the U. S. foursome of John Kinsella, Fred Tyler, Steve Genter and Spitz lined up for the 800-meter free-style relay. It was a Yankee triumph all the way, and Spitz touched out on his anchor leg at 7:35.78—more than eight seconds under the old world record. Mark Spitz's five golds had now tied the mark of Italy's Nedo Nadi.

On September 3, the experts were saying that the lithe, 6-foot Spitz would have a tough time keeping his now-famous mustache out in front in the 100-meter free-style.

Spitz had strained his back getting out of a small car the day before, and no one knew how much the injury would hamper him. In the qualifying heats he had been content to swim second to Australia's Mike Wenden. Had the injury slowed him down—or was he just saving his strength for the final?

America's Jerry Heidenreich, a great sprinter, was determined to end Spitz's streak. But Mark took off like a torpedo. Although Heidenreich trailed by only a few feet, he never caught the speedy Spitz whose 51.22 gave him his sixth world record and his sixth gold.

Now on September 4, only the 400-meter medley relay was left—the finale of the swimming program. Backstroker Mike Stam and breaststroker Tom Bruce combined to give a two-foot lead to Spitz, who was swimming the third leg, the 100-meter butterfly. His arched body slammed into the water and his long, strong arms swooped up, over and under in the butterfly. Water flowed over his head and powerful shoulders as he swam the greatest 'fly leg of his life and gave Jerry Heidenreich a twelve-foot lead on the anchor leg. Heidenreich breezed home, increasing the lead to 15 feet, for a new world record of 3:48.16.

As the four Americans stood on the victory stand, Mark Spitz, the world's greatest swimmer, was wearing his seventh gold medal. Olympic fans had never seen anything like it.

With his seventh medal around his neck, the new celebrity waves to his admirers.

44

Billie Jean Slays a Dragon

There had been great names in women's tennis before—such as Helen Wills, Alice Marble, Althea Gibson, little Mo Connolly and others. But nobody ever startled the tennis world the way Billie Jean King did on the night of September 20, 1973, in the Astrodome in Houston.

Billie Jean, the reigning Queen of the Courts, was going to play Bobby Riggs, a tennis "hustler" who had been national men's singles champion 30 years earlier.

At 55, Riggs was still a fine player who was making a good living by betting on his own game in private matches. He would play a less skilled opponent under almost any handicap—giving up points or playing with an open umbrella in one hand or wearing heavy rubber boots. With money on the line, Bobby almost never lost. He was too old to rely on speed and stamina, but he was a master at placing his shots, lobbing them over an opponent's head or loading the ball with spin, causing it to bounce erratically.

In 1973 the women in professional tennis began speaking out, demanding more prize money and more attention. Riggs put down women's tennis as a patty-cake game. They didn't deserve more money, he said. At age 55, he could beat the best woman player in the world.

One word led to another; boast piled upon boast. The trap was being baited. Margaret Smith Court, the Australian star and Wimbledon champion, was the first woman to snap at it. She and Riggs agreed to meet for a two-out-of-three set match, for a purse of $10,000, winner take all.

The match was played on Mother's Day 1973. For weeks Bobby had been wondering out loud how Margaret Court would do in "the most important match of her life."

The dragon: boastful 55-year-old Bobby Riggs jumps over the net held down by Ms. King.

As the players met at courtside, he presented her with a bouquet of roses, and Mrs. Court curtsied. The pressure, the publicity and Riggs' unaccustomed gallantry seemed to throw her off her game. Riggs took control at the start and blew her off the court in straight sets, 6–2, 6–1.

Riggs' comments about women's tennis became more barbed than ever. Now he went after the only woman who might be better than Margaret Smith Court.

As a California tomboy, Billie Jean Moffitt had developed a tough, competitive spirit. Her brother, Randy, later became a major league pitcher, and although Billie Jean played baseball with the boys on the block, tennis was her game.

At 18, she stunned the tennis world by upsetting Margaret Smith, the defending champion, in a second round match at Wimbledon. The following year she carried Miss Smith to the finals and lost.

In the next few years Billie Jean (who became Billie Jean King when she married) battled Margaret Smith Court for the title of world's greatest woman player. She was U.S. singles champion three times and Wimbledon champion five times.

In the summer of 1973, on her way to becoming the first woman athlete to earn $100,000 in a year, Billie Jean agreed to meet Bobby Riggs. She had been the most outspoken of the women players in demand-

ing equal attention for women's tennis, and now she had a chance to avenge the defeat of Margaret Court. King and Riggs would play the best three-of-five match and the winner would take home $100,000.

It all happened on September 20, 1973, in Houston's Astrodome, and 30,492 people —the largest crowd ever to see a tennis match—flocked to see it, some of them paying as much as $100 for court-side tickets. Television beamed the contest to 36 nations besides the U.S., and it was estimated that more than 40,000,000 people tuned in.

As a brass band blared from a spot behind home plate and the television cameras searched for celebrities in the crowd, Billie Jean was brought to court-side on a Cleopatra-style gold litter, held up by four

The challenger: women's champion Billie Jean King, one of the game's great competitors.

muscled athletes from Rice University. Then Riggs appeared in a gold-wheeled rickshaw, pulled by six dazzling models in red and gold outfits.

The whole event had the atmosphere of a carnival, but millions were also interested in the basic question: could a great woman player beat a 55-year-old man? The question was answered in just two hours and four minutes.

Billie Jean served first. She played cautiously and won the first game rather easily. They changed service, and Riggs ran off four straight points to win the second game. Then he won three more with Billie Jean serving. That was it, many fans figured. Here comes Bobby and there goes Billie. The male was still superior to the female.

But Billie Jean was just warming up. After those seven straight points for Riggs she moved swiftly to attack. She drove Bobby to the far corners of the court, running back and forth along the baselines. She hit low volleys at his feet. She destroyed his famous lobs. Her chief tools were the tools of men's tennis: the serve and volley. Her service came so hard that Bobby was on the defensive, and he was helpless when she rushed the net and slammed the ball past him.

There was a look of calm but steely determination on Billie Jean King's face as she smashed, and slashed, darting over the court to reach everything Riggs could send back at her.

She demolished Riggs in three straight sets, 6-4, 6-3, 6-3. But the amazing thing about her victory was the fact that 70 of the 109 points she scored were outright winners —shots which Riggs never even touched.

When Riggs double-faulted into the net to give Billie Jean match point in the third and final set it was all over. He barely had enough strength left to leap the net to congratulate her. Billie Jean King raised her racquet high and made a fist with her other hand.

The winner in three straight sets is a proud and happy Billie Jean.

In front of TV sets around the world, women cheered a new heroine, a spokeswoman for women's equality. Meanwhile, millions of men watched with sympathy as Bobby Riggs, his muscles aching and his boasting silenced, limped away in defeat.

Index

ABOUT THE AUTHOR

Jerry Brondfield is a veteran sportswriter, director of film documentaries and editor. He is a graduate of Ohio State University and has served that school as an unpaid football recruiter for over twenty years. A frequent contributor to *Reader's Digest* and other national publications, he is also the author of several sports books for young readers and adults. His most recent book is *Woody Hayes and the 100-Yard War* (1974), a portrait of the controversial Ohio State football coach. Mr. Brondfield is an editor for Scholastic Magazines and lives in Roslyn Heights, New York.

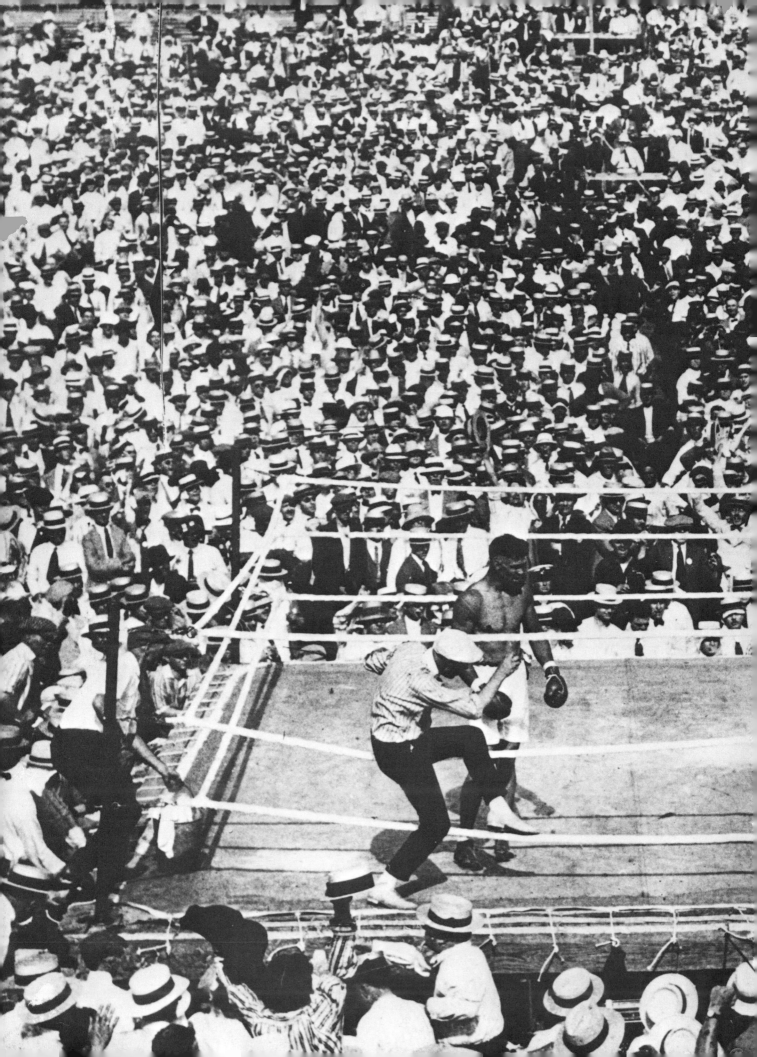